VIA Folios 164

The Mercury Man

REMEMBERING BROOKLYN

© 2023, Frank Gioia

ORIGINAL COVER AND BOOK DESIGN
The Troy Book Makers • Troy, New York • thetroybookmakers.com

COVER IMAGE
178a Schaefer St., Brooklyn
©Municipal Archives, City of New York

Library of Congress Control Number: 2023940207

Published by
BORDIGHERA PRESS
John D. Calandra Italian American Institute
25 W. 43rd Street, 17th Floor
New York, NY 10036

VIA Folios 164
ISBN 978-1-59954-198-3

THE MERCURY MAN

REMEMBERING BROOKLYN

Frank Gioia

BORDIGHERA PRESS

This work is dedicated to my guys
Tony Augugliaro, John Flore and Billy Candotti.

We tried to take care of each other

When you look into the eyes of another,
you look into the eyes of God.

A variation on scripture by Rabbi Alan Berg

Table of Contents

Introduction

I have put this collection of short stories together to give voice to what I've come to embrace as the defining period of my life. My formative years, a time when friendships filled in for the broken family of my childhood. In these narratives, I have been able to revisit and experience the rich texture of an earlier time and place. These are my recollections of growing up on the streets of Brooklyn in an Italian working-class family in the 1950s and early '60s. Some of these pieces also evoke memories of my time in the army and the year I spent in Vietnam. Here is what transpired as I passed from being a boy to becoming a man.

I hope these words bring about some understanding of my journey.

Food for Thought

We were going sixty, seventy, and then eighty miles an hour. Fast, faster, fastest. My mother's window open, she, looking out and saying to no one in particular, "I love the breeze." The '49 Buick Special flying down the Southern State, chrome glistening as the sun peeked over the horizon. The excitement palpable in the early morning chill. My father always in the lead, followed by my uncles, Charlie and Nick, in their GM cars, as we raced to Alley Pond Park. Leaving home at 6 a.m., to beat the traffic. Man, could Uncle Charlie dance! Great balance. He taught me to ride a bike when I was still struggling at age ten. I remember him doing the Charleston and the jitterbug at football weddings. Those celebrations from the '50s where the men used to throw ready-made sandwiches to one another. They would just yell, "Nino, a capicola sandwich please." And the guy would do his best Johnny Unitas and throw a pass. Uncle Nick was a natty dresser. You could cut your fingers on the crease of his pants. He wore chambray shirts, never linen. He would make these fashion statements like "Linen never looks fresh. No matter how much you press it, it always looks wrinkled." He would know. He stood over a steam iron all day and pressed garments for a living. He also liked to remind us kids that you couldn't wear white after Labor Day. That went for shoes as well as pants. My father was also a clothes horse. Spent as much time in front of the mirror as my mother. He had a collection of rayon shirts the colors of ice cream. My mother spent long afternoons bent over an ironing board, listening to Dean Martin and Sinatra, pressing those pastel-colored shirts, as well as his T-shirts, handkerchiefs, and boxer shorts. Underwear needed to lie flat against the body, not interfere with the pleats of his pants.

At the park, we would commandeer our favorite picnic spot near the lake. Playing catch, throwing a football, maybe a softball game if all the cousins showed up. But it was mostly about the eating. Bagels and cream cheese, with a meatball on the side. Not one on top of the other, but together on the same paper plate. A little something to keep us going while we emptied the cars and set up camp. Our car held the pizzas, white only for my grandfather, topped with bread crumb, anchovies, and olive oil. And the rice balls, *arancini*. White rice, shaped like a baseball and filled with ground veal, peas, and tomato, rolled in bread crumbs and fried. My mother's specialty. Her claim to fame. My uncles would tell her, "Ro, nobody makes them like you," and her face would light up like our new TV screen. But not until my father got home from work and turned it on. We weren't allowed to touch it. The phone either. Those were the rules until I was twelve . . . when my father left us. From Aunt Josie came trays of manicotti and lasagna. She made cheese dance, like my Uncle Charlie could Lindy. Aunt Fay made the parmigiana. Eggplant, not veal, because Uncle Nick knew how to stretch a buck, and even then a pound of veal was beyond a presser's reach. The coolers filled to the top with soda, beer, and enough sausage to open a pork store. Every Italian neighborhood had at least one. A store devoted exclusively to commerce in pig. The traditional bacon, chops, and ribs of course. But also pickled feet, caul fat, and pork skin. The skin my mother used to make braciola. Filled with onions, pine nuts, raisins, salami, and hard-boiled eggs. Floating in tomato sauce and slowly releasing its cholesterol. Should Brooklyn be attacked in our absence, we would survive. We carried large pots and black frying pans that had made the trip from the mother country. Salads, olive oil, and vinegar. Watermelons and peaches bought from the black man with the horse-drawn wagon. In the trunk of our car were cases of Redpack tomatoes. Boxes of Ronzoni pasta. No. 8, because no matter what, on Sunday the men had to have their spaghetti. What do they work all week for anyway? These picnics were celebrations, a way to show how well these men were doing. How hard they worked and how much they cared for their families.

Joy was everywhere. My dad looking at my mom with his flirty grin. My mom returning his affection with a demure look. My aunts, happily setting the wooden tables. My uncles whistling as they cleaned the grills to cook their sausages. We kids running down to the beach to catch frogs. Go for a swim. The anticipation and the laughter infecting the early morning air. Then I heard my father say, "Of course they're coming, Tony and Betty. They should be here soon." And my mother, knowing how my father looked at my aunt, tried to smile. Her voice no longer bubbly, sounding like the air had been let out of a balloon. She tried to speak but couldn't find the words. She caught her breath, but again, no words came out. I felt the hair stand up on my arms. "Don't cry, ma. Please don't cry."

Down on the Corner

We were playing two on two in the playground when they came through the gates. There were three of them. We hadn't seen them before, though they would've been hard to miss. One wore garrison boots and had a bandana wrapped around his head. The other two carried umbrellas and were wearing stingy-brim hats on a bright, sunny day. They were about sixteen. We were probably thirteen, the summer before high school. Asked if they could play.

They said their names were Benny, Bobby, and Whitey. That they hung out in Halsey Park, where my grandfather and his *paisans* met every morning. To talk about the Old Country, remember those gone by. They wanted to know how tough we were. Could each of us kick the shit out of two guys? Had we heard of the Halsey Bops? What about the Saints, those punks from Queens, or those Italian boys from Fulton and Rockaway? Whitey wanted to know, "Had we been with girls . . . or were we pulling it?" He laughed. Took out his switchblade and jumped around a little like Zorro. "Were we maybe a bit crazy like him?"

Me and some of the guys met up with them in the park that night. Sat together on the wooden benches, transistors blasting, and passed around bottles of cold beer and warm Thunderbird. Groups singing doo-wop. Couples making out. Benny and Whitey talked about the bazaar at 14 Holy Martyrs that weekend. Wanted to know if we could get ten guys together. They had heard the Corsair Lords were trying to push past Broadway, move into our neighborhood. Bushwick was our turf. They said we needed to send them a message. Protect our block from the black guys and the Puerto Ricans. At around eleven, some of the older guys started to get into cars. There was going to be drag racing down by the church. I was supposed to be home by ten, but there was no way I was going to miss this. Bobby, who looked young to be driving, got behind the wheel of a '55 Ford convertible, decked out with fender skirts and Hollywood mufflers. Then these two girls from school, JoJo and Ann Marie, dressed in pedal pushers and tight sweaters and wearing makeup to look older, got in beside him. They were really cool, and when I mentioned my graduation party, they said they'd be there with bells on. Maybe even bring some booze. I ran into them again a few years later, and they were running a business in the park. It looked like business was very, very good.

Down on Central, it was like a party. The noise from at least a dozen cars revving up, sometimes backfiring. Guys were high-fiving each other, the girls leaning in the open windows and kissing their boyfriends. The race was about a block long, in front of the school, down the corner from my house. The streets had been closed off for a couple of blocks in each direction. Whitey stood at the starting line and held a white flag he had picked up from a construction site. Benny was at the finish line and would call the winner. I remember looking at Bobby and thinking how good looking he was. I had heard him say he wanted to become a model. It surprised me because I thought only girls became models.

On Saturday night a group of us hooked up with the Bops again at the bazaar. Stood around watching Joe Z, a local grifter, late-bet the roulette wheel, stuff his pocket with twenties. Then we noticed the black guys in small groups of two and three. Before anyone knew what was happening, this tall, skinny cat knocked over one of the roulette tables. Tried to steal some quarters, but me and Tony were on him before he could make his move. I was still on the ground, enjoying the moment, when the Lords reacted and quickly got the upper hand. How did I get here, I thought? My heart racing, afraid I might get stomped. But in no time, Johnny Boy and his crew from Fulton and Rockaway—this is years before Johnny became a Mafia boss—jumped in and saved my ass. Chased the motherfuckers down Central and back toward Broadway. Later, me and some of the guys walked over to Halsey Park. Whitey took out his switchblade, and we all cut ourselves. Then we took turns swapping blood. We were in. Halsey Bops for life.

Here Comes Kenny

He always drove down the block very slowly, checking to see if anyone was around. It wasn't a new car. He kept it nice though. A two-tone, green-and-white '49 Oldsmobile. It had a shiny metal visor over the windshield, whitewall tires, and a chrome bumper that looked like a barracuda. Kenny always showed up after dinner. He would come around about once a week and take us for rides to Highland Park or to play miniature golf. Sometimes, if he liked you, to the movies. He liked John a lot.

John always sat in the front seat of the big Olds 98. It allowed Kenny lots of room to reach over and touch his leg when he let him. The rest of us squeezed into the rear of the two-door sedan, trying to watch what was going on up front. Ken wore false teeth, which he removed before John let him do anything. Usually, he would drive to the park and give us a fiver to spend at the concession stand. Then he would give John another five after John let him do it. He just had to sit there while Kenny played with him, went down on him . . . until he came. He sold insurance during the day, bought young boys at night. We were like thirteen or fourteen, he was probably around thirty-five. Not a bad-looking guy. I'm sure he could have gotten lots of girls if he had wanted to, except he liked boys. Dark and thin, with curly black hair. I was dark and had black hair, but I was fat, so I didn't interest him.

Nobody used the word gay then. Ken was a homo, at least that's what we called him. They said he lived with his mother over on Myrtle. In Queens. There was a Chinese restaurant he took us to once. The Shanghai Palace or something like that. It might have been the first time I had been in a restaurant without my parents. It was a Friday night, and there was going to be entertainment. Ken explained that the entertainers would perform numbers from the great American songbook. Like Broadway. A revue, he called it, but in drag. I was still eating my chicken chow mein and thinking about what he had said when six of the most beautiful women, wearing fishnet stockings and dressed to the nines, started singing onstage. Then two of these women, dressed like Marilyn Monroe and Jane Russell, did a duet of "Diamonds Are a Girl's Best Friend," which Kenny said was from a movie out a couple of years before called *Gentlemen Prefer Blondes*. Looking at them, I started to get excited and had to be sure to keep my legs under the table.

I thought of this years later, hanging out on Tu Do Street in Saigon. Billie and I were at the Hollywood Bar. The bar girls, or B-girls, as they were called, sharing our couch and our money. Dressed to look like Marilyn and Jane. Stars we knew from the movies and from calendars. Doing the hard work of trying to get us to buy them the overpriced, whiskey-colored tea they were served whenever a soldier bought them a drink. The mama-san in charge keeping an eye on them. Making sure their makeup was fresh, the seam of their nylons straight. That they took full advantage of the situation. Whispering while they licked your ear. Placing your hand in the slit of their dress so you could move it up their leg. So they could tease you with the feel of a soft thigh. Making sure you never got as far as the crotch. All the while asking for another drink and promising some late-night reward. "GI like Jane? Like Jane take you home?" Another lick, a giggle. "Only 10,000 P." About $70 bucks at the 1960s black market exchange rate.

You wondered then if this was a situation similar to that night at the Chinese restaurant. A repeat of the drag show. I mean, they looked like girls. Beautiful. Soft hair, exquisite breasts, and long legs. But what if they were guys? Could this be just another show? I remembered how it ended that night at the Palace. How they took their wigs off, and everyone laughed and clapped like crazy. And how I had gotten hard. What if these girls were guys? How would you know?

Fat Boy

Not sure when it first started, but definitely by the time I was in third grade in grammar school. "Hey, fat boy, ya wanna play stickball?" It was the kids in the schoolyard, around the time I first started keeping my shirttails out. To cover my behind. Man, I loved to eat. And my aunts, my mom, they would always be feeding me. "Eat, Frankie. Take more. It's good, huh?" Then it was picked up by the guys I hung with after school, my guys from the block. That's when it became harder. We had just started to think about girls. Playing kissing games like spin the bottle. And fat was not in, not for young boys or girls. It made me feel kind of helpless and angry. It was impossible to control what other people said about me. If I lashed out every time somebody called me fat, I would be fighting all day long. As it was, there were enough situations where I reacted and would knock a guy to the ground because he made some wisecrack about my ass. Then I would twist his arm until he took it back. The entire situation pissed me off. It hurt to go hungry, and when I tried to diet, I would only be successful for a day or two. Then I would begin eating again, second and third helpings of pasta, or snack on cookies and ice cream in front of the TV. As I got older, guys used the fat word as payback for something I had done to them. Maybe I made a mother joke or called them stupid because they failed a spelling test. I would remember, though, and get my revenge by not picking them when we chose up sides for one of our countless stickball games.

I was always a captain. Would just talk my way into it. If anyone complained, I would just say, "Fuck you, what're you gonna do about it?" Then toss my bat to John and say, "Choose." We would play out the hand-over-hand ritual to see who ended up with the knob. If he did, I got a chance to kick the bat out of his hand. If he held on, he chose first. If not, I did. Even though I was heavy, I was graceful. I could hit and field as well as anyone. And I was blessed with good hands. Maybe not as good as John, who was definitely the star player on our block, but nearly everyone else. It was because I couldn't run for shit that the guys figured out other ways to tease me.

The Wilson Avenue station on the BMT Canarsie line was a few blocks from my house. About the same distance as the Chauncey Street stop on the Broadway elevated line. Wilson was the neighborhood, Broadway not so much. If you took the El to get home, you had to walk down Broadway. It was the boundary between the white and black neighborhoods, and you only went there if you were in a group. If you were alone, guys would talk shit to you. "Hey, white boy, what the fuck you doin here? You lost or somethin?" Up until high school, I wasn't very confident on the subways. Trains on both sides of the tracks. Dark tunnels, screaming decibels. Upstairs, downstairs. Local, express. BMT, IND. Run, wait, hurry, the doors are closing. Get on. No, let's take the next one. The subways freaked me out. A total loss of control.

There was the day we had gone to Cypress pool, over on Jamaica Avenue. That was enough of a challenge. Wearing a bathing suit. Casually adjusting the waistband, trying to keep my hips from spilling outside the suit. On the way home, we had to change trains at Eastern Parkway. To confuse me, all the guys began running in different directions. I didn't know whom to follow, and I couldn't keep up with them. Then I saw them laughing on the other side of the tracks. I was on the wrong side of the platform and didn't know how to cross over. I felt so alone. I wanted to kill the motherfuckers. After that, I transferred to the El by mistake. Walking down Broadway, I was the only white person on the street. People were looking at me, and after a few blocks I started to get nervous. So I ducked into a White Castle. For a burger and an order of fries.

Halsey Bops

There were short men and tall, others fat, and some with hair but mostly bald. Dressed in heavy dark suits and shiny wide ties covering their fraying white shirts with long pointy collars. Old men all, they sat on the wooden benches with fedoras on their heads, in all kinds of weather, and talked in a language soon to be forgotten. They arrived in the morning after school had begun and talked about days that now seemed like dreams. They scattered for lunch, having mourned the departed, and returned after napping to stake their claim to a park that was theirs, but only until the school bells rang.

Newly arrived at the turn of the century from Sicily, they had migrated to the Bushwick section of Brooklyn. A strong back earned them work in the breweries, the factories, and the construction trades. The more enterprising renting storefronts and working as cobblers, and bakers, and butchers, and takers. They approached life's end with social security checks to put food on the table, but absent love from their children, who spent the weekends polishing their Pontiacs and dreaming of the model homes in Levittown. As their numbers diminished, their voices on the wooden benches were replaced by the transistor sounds of the Moonglows, the Flamingos, and the Platters. Their grandchildren took the B26 bus on Halsey Street to the Brooklyn Paramount to cheer the black doo-wop groups, while at the same time creating gangs to protect the neighborhood from them. The Halsey Bops, the Ellery Bops, and Fulton and Rockaway, an early John Gotti proving ground, were made up of Italian and Irish guys who defended their turf and fought to maintain the racial purity that existed on our side of Broadway.

The black gangs were the Bishops, even though they skipped being ordained in the Catholic Church, and the Chaplains, who lived in the projects in Bed-Stuy. Gang fights could be called for almost any reason. We had one when our bus was attacked returning from downtown Brooklyn. Its open windows left us exposed as chunks of concrete stuffed into dirty old socks became weapons against anyone with the misfortune of having gotten a good seat by a window. A couple of guys had been bloodied, but it was over quickly and the bus resumed its journey to a more friendly location. Only the Chaplains would have the balls to do that. They would have to be taught a lesson. We couldn't be targeted every time we needed to get through their turf to buy a couple of button-downs, or go to a rock-and-roll show.

That afternoon, prior to the attack, had been a mindfuck. An Alan Freed show with Little Richard as the headliner. In the middle of his act, with the place packed, chicks screaming and the balcony rocking, my man Sammy had given Richard a sign. The sign said Little Richard for President, and when Richard held it up, the place went wild. People were dancing in the aisles and jumping on their seats. The cops lost control, and they threw Sammy out. Little Richard stopped the show. Refused to perform any longer until they brought Sammy back in. Now these motherfuckers had knocked Sammy upside his head. We would have to respond, big-time. Let them know they couldn't fuck with the Halsey Bops.

The rumble was set for dark the following Friday. Everything was in, including zip guns. The Chaplains chose the playground at PS 113. We agreed, not to entertain Jackie Gleason's mother, who still lived around the corner, but because we could approach unseen from the dead end in back of the subway station. We would be waiting for them when they arrived. We spent the week talking shit, sharpening weapons, and collecting beer bottles to make gasoline bombs. Gang fights were usually more about posturing than actual fighting, so our greeting their arrival with six-packs of fire raining through the night sky shocked us almost as much as them. As they scattered, we ran after them with baseball bats. Then, as if appearing from nowhere, a large black dude in a white robe made his way through the chaos. At first no one challenged him. Then the fighting stopped, and we watched as he and Benny began to go at it like two actors in an Errol

Flynn movie. It was pure ballet, if not for the knives and the fact that they were trying to kill each other. In an instant, red flashing lights ricocheted in the night sky, and New York's finest were on the scene. Together we stood, legs forced apart, both light and dark faces, staring at the crimson brick wall. The men in blue, the object of our mutual scorn. Sweat mixed with laughter, and our camaraderie developed during a hell-raising ride to the 83rd Precinct in the back of a paddy wagon.

Since most of us hadn't yet reached a sweet sixteen, we were released before midnight with only a warning. Color blind, we returned to the neighborhood, where an obliging wino helped us secure the finest in cheap liquid refreshments. Someone grabbed a bag of Italian bread left for a pickup at the bakery, and we headed for Halsey Park. There we spent the night, breaking bread, drinking wine, and telling ego-driven stories designed to prove who had the biggest cock.

Get a Job

Aunt Marion, my cousin Lefty's mom, was deeply religious. Attended the 6:30 mass every morning at St. Barbara's over on Bleecker Street. Deep in the heart of Bushwick, near the chicken market. Where every so often she would pick up a couple of skinned rabbits for a special Sunday dinner. Roast *coniglio,* with sea salt and green olives. She walked over a mile to church instead of going to St. Martin of Tours, a few blocks from the family home on Putnam. Preferred to sit with the three or four other Italian ladies, dressed all in black. To hear the words of God from Father Conte, rather than trying to understand the brogue of Father Sweeney. She was convinced that by going to mass every day and praying to what she called "the Almighty," she would remain in a state of grace and escape the evil eye of the devil. The *maloik* or *malocchio,* as every good Sicilian knew, was a curse to be avoided. Better to spend your time praying to the Lord, increase your chances of remaining in his good graces, and cut down on the possibility that you could wind up in hell for all eternity.

After being on her knees for half an hour, extolling the virtues of God, she would reward herself with a nickel ride on the trolley for the return trip home, to make coffee for my Uncle Jimmy. Then they would catch the subway into the city and their jobs in the garment center. Pretty much everyone in my family was employed in the rag trade. Uncle Jim and my father—Aunt Marion was the oldest of his two sisters—both drove trucks between the sweatshops in Brooklyn and the fashion showrooms high above the streets of Manhattan. When our families got together, they would make fun of my aunt's pronouncements about the all-knowing God and his ability to see and hear everything from up there. Once I went to their house to see Lefty and I heard her praying through the open bedroom window.

"Dearest and most merciful God," she said. "Creator of all that is good and holy, remember us, your humble servants. Bless us, and shine perpetual light upon us." This was in sixth grade, when I was around eleven years old and a student at 14 Holy Martyrs. It was during the time I was studying to be confirmed. Where, on a given Sunday morning, you say a few prayers, a bishop from the diocese blesses you and then smacks you across the face, a little too hard. Just like that you become a soldier in God's army, no physical exam even. I had asked Lefty to be my godfather, not because he was religious like his mom, but because I knew she would take this observance seriously and front him a few bucks, if necessary, so he could buy me a nice gift to mark the occasion. Which, of course, he did.

During the lead-up to this event, the church pastor would constantly remind the boys in our class that we should be thinking about what we could do to live more meaningful lives. How we could better serve God. That we should consider becoming priests. My Uncle Jim suggested that I could become a toll taker. "Steady work," he said. "You listen to the radio all day, take people's quarters." Did I really want to be listening to Jack Spector, Top-40 all day? "Ya know," he continued, "you could think about becoming a garbage man. If you can pass the test." These were city jobs, he told me. With pensions, which seemed to be an important selling point. I never could figure out why you needed to take a test to collect someone's garbage. And besides, there was no fucking way I was going to spend my life picking up other people's shit. No, I liked the direction that Lefty was going. Hanging out in that bar and grill down on Knickerbocker. Vito's place. Where he hung out with this guy, Skinny Vinny, who always wore a suit, no tie, and carried a roll of fifties big enough to choke a horse. I liked the idea of going to work in a suit. Stopping by the bootblack every morning to get my featherweights polished. Two bits. Fifteen cents for the shine guy and a dime for the tip. Let them get their hands dirty. I liked having clean nails.

How to Buy Real Estate

When I was about eight years old, my parents took me to a summer gathering at a house near John's Pizzeria in Brooklyn. It was a large Italian neighborhood, with many newly arrived immigrants, that stretched to the fringes of Williamsburg. "Uncle" John and my father were close boyhood friends, and he sometimes took me there on Monday nights when the restaurant was closed. It was a time for the men to get together, eat and play pinochle. Daydreaming, I recalled going in the kitchen the previous week to watch as Uncle John prepared the *capuzzelle*. First, he removed the split lamb heads from a large pot of boiling water and laid them out to dry on rectangular trays that were used to make Sicilian pizza. He inserted slivers of garlic, sprinkled them with olive oil and finished the preparation with salt, pepper, and oregano. They were then roasted in the wood-fired oven. Sizzling hot, the lamb heads were served with a wedge of lemon, a dish of pasta *aglio e olio,* and a salad. Each of the heads contained some of the succulent meat, a row of small teeth, and one half of the brain. I was reluctant to try it, but the men encouraged me, and as I ate from my father's fork, I heard him say, *Mangia,* Frankie, eat. This is food from the gods."

The party was at a six-family house on Harman Street that had recently been purchased by relatives from my mother's ancestral village in Sicily, Santa Margherita di Belice. I followed along with my grandfather, my father, and the other men as they looked at the building and debated whether it was a good piece of real estate. The exterior was made of red brick, and I learned that day that brick was the preferred building material of my people. It could not be blown down, did not have to be painted, and if a repair happened to be necessary and you knew a goombah in construction, a trunkful of brick could easily be obtained by slipping a five spot to the guard at a building site.

The basement was cavernous, and the large foundation stones had been whitewashed. The homeowner and his two sons had recently poured a cement floor, of which he was very proud. Then I heard him say you could *"mangiare dal pavimento."* I thought about this and how my mother would encourage us to pick up food we had dropped on the kitchen floor and ask for God's blessing before eating it. What she called "kissing it up to God." When we reached the end of the basement, the bulkhead doors were open and wooden crates with gaily printed pictures of children playing in the countryside stood against the wall. Standing there, in a makeshift wooden tub, barefoot and with their pants rolled to their knees, were the man's two sons, Vincent and Carmine. They were laughing as they emptied the boxes and stomped on the grapes to make wine. I had never seen anyone make wine before and asked if I could give it a try. My grandfather smiled and assured his *paisan* my feet were clean. Then he lied and told him my mother made sure I bathed every day. So after removing my shoes and socks and rolling up my dungarees, I joined the dance until my feet were purple and I got bored.

Next, we went into the yard and sat at a table where large platters with gold rims were piled high with grilled sausages, roasted peppers, and onions. A pear-shaped provolone, with the twine still attached for when it hung to cure, sat on a butcher block nearby. One of the man's sons generously carved chunks from the cheese and passed them around. My grandfather, who owned his own apartment house, ripped off an end from a loaf of bread, bit into his cheese and said to his countryman, *"Nunziato, quanto tua casa?"* The man explained in broken English that his family lived in one apartment and he rented the others for an average of $40 a month. My grandfather quickly added up the rents in his head and came up with a round figure of $2,900 in annual rent. That meant the house was worth approximately $14,500. A good real estate deal should pay for itself in five years, he said. The man wished that were the case, but the apartments were rented to poor relatives from *la patria*. He only charged what people could afford. Unfortunately, he had paid too much. I thought about the apartments, stacked one on top of the other and the split heads laid one above the other on the trays. All I could think about was my reader from first grade, "Mary Had a Little Lamb."

Christmas Eve

The big, black Buick, as if driving itself, floated over the trolley tracks on Wilson Avenue. Fat, fluffy, snowflakes fell silently, and the bells from St. Martin's tolled in the background. In the rear, my brother Joe and I sank into the cushy mohair seats. In the front, my mother's pleading broke the silence. "Why, Jerry why? Why do you have to work on Christmas Eve? Nobody works on Christmas." My father, in his calm, controlling voice, said that he had a trunkful of suits and dresses. The latest in women's fashion. If he sold a few things, he could make as much as fifty bucks. Besides, the money would come in handy for the holidays. We would have dinner at Aunt Marion's, then he would go to Uncle Tony and Aunt Betty's in Hempstead. He'd be back by midnight. "C'mon, doll," he crooned, "Let's not get into a fight. You'll scare the kids."

While my father parked the Buick, I considered the suits. Although he drove a truck for a living, I had recently become aware that my father was a thief. Not a real crook like you read about in the *Daily News,* but something he did to earn extra money. He would steal a suit or dress while making a delivery to a factory, and after work he would sell them to friends or relatives for their wives or girlfriends or both.

The house sparkled for the holidays. A Christmas tree in the window, flashing lights around the doors. As we entered, my Uncle Jimmy yelled, "Frankie, come and sit next to your uncle. Let's have a cherry." The cherries sat drowning in whiskey. Chivas Regal, for the holidays. My Aunt Marion kissed me as I passed her, wooden spoon in hand, stirring a large pot of fava beans. I hugged my Aunt Rosie while she fondled the pastries, her huge breasts splayed across the kitchen table. Not for nothing was she known as Titty Rosie.

"What's the matter?" my Aunt Rosie asked my mom. My mother, unable to hide her disappointment, said, "It's Jerry. He's going to Tony and Betty's later, says he has to work." "My brother Tony's working too," my aunt replied.

I eagerly took the shot glass holding the forbidden fruit from my Uncle Jimmy. Looking skyward, my Aunt Marion murmured a prayer, and I slipped the cherry past my lips. The heat of the alcohol traveled from my throat into my stomach and then down to my crotch. My eyes closed, and my thoughts shifted to my Aunt Betty. I had first seen her naked this past summer. We had dropped by their apartment so we could drive in tandem to Brighton Beach. I had gone into the bedroom to ask about my bathing suit, and she and my mom were changing. When I saw her, she smiled and continued sliding her long, shaved leg into her bathing suit. My mother, who until then was the only woman I had ever seen naked, was very attractive. Aunt Betty was off the charts. An absolute knockout, like a Madonna with heat. I remembered the way my father looked at her. His smirk, the way he kept his eyes on her when she walked by. I couldn't take my eyes off her, and apparently neither could he. I watched as the suit covered her round breasts and the large brown nipples disappeared. Burnt umber, I remembered the color from my Crayola set. Even though I had not yet reached puberty, I had what I've always thought of as my first sexual experience.

The heat in my crotch transferred to my upper arms as Lefty greeted me with a right jab and a left hook. He put his arms around my shoulders, squeezed hard and bit my cheek. Lefty's attention was affection to the max. He always made me feel special, and I loved that he was happy to see me. He was my coolest relative, and on this Christmas Eve 1952, he was dressed to kill. Powder-blue, pegged pants hugged shiny leather wingtips, and the duck's ass on his neck caressed his rayon shirt. His girlfriend, Mary, who the adults said looked like Cyd Charisse, lounged on the sofa, and Lefty's Golden Gloves trophy sat on a mantle nearby. He was a charmer, and though still in his teens, everyone except his mother treated him like a man. Some years later he took me to eat in Little Italy. Mussels in spicy tomato sauce and hard biscuits. We sipped whiskey as he did his business. Men in suits with white envelopes and prominent inside pockets came by to pay their respects. It was heady stuff, and I wondered if that was my future.

For dinner, long, narrow tables were arranged end to end, covered with white cotton sheets and set with the best family china. Extending from the kitchen to the parlor, the tables quickly became filled with great-uncles with great stomachs, women in rouge and rhinestones, and screaming cousins. The eating continued as relatives hugged, kissed and stretched across the table for mushrooms stuffed with *muddica,* octopus swimming in olive oil, fried eel, and *arancini.* At around 8 p.m., the lobster tails were slipped under the broiler, and chicken soup with orzo was served. Tradition dictated that no meat, but at least seven fish courses, be eaten before the sausage at midnight. Seven being the most repeated number in the Bible. After feasting on the main courses, we followed with cannoli, *cassata,* and cups of demitasse. Roasted nuts, fruit, and the whiskey-soaked cherries littered the table until 12 o'clock at night. Then it was time to eat the sausage. My father, true to his plan, left for Hempstead after the lobster. Even though he promised us, we didn't see him again until the next morning. I wondered if the pink dress fit my Aunt Betty. Did she ask him to zip up the back when she modeled it for him?

Make-Believe Sergeant

We were standing around making small talk, trying not to look scared, when the captain walked into the room. One of the two sergeants bullshitting in the corner jumped up and shouted for us to line up, stand at attention. The captain, wearing his dress uniform and looking like he just stepped out of a recruiting poster, smiled and said, "Good morning, gentlemen. Please repeat after me: 'I do solemnly swear that I will support and defend.'" All of a sudden I couldn't focus. I was having trouble breathing. As if someone had his hands on my throat. I was choking. Did I take the oath? My mouth moved, but I'm not sure if any words came out. It didn't matter, because I was definitely screwed. The other sergeant started screaming, "Next, next," and I heard buzzing in my ears. In seconds, my hair was on the floor. My dark, wavy hair, pompadour and sideburns. Gone. My best body part. History.

We had taken the train downtown to Whitehall Street. The subway tunnel all grime and no longer white tile in a long straight line. The noise of the trains clashing with the noise in my brain. Christmas lights flashing, calling to anyone with an unfinished shopping list. Churches pumping out hymns like a broken soundtrack. Why had I listened to that fucking recruiter? Conned the shit out of me. Tony and Billy were joining the army, and he explained how we could all go in together, the buddy plan. We would be stationed at Fort Dix in New Jersey. We could go home on weekends. My mom thought I was kidding. Just some joke I was running. But this was for real, not like when I asked her if I could join the Boy Scouts, go away for the weekend.

We were issued big green bags. Duffels to carry all the shit in. Man, the thing was heavy. Everything dark green. No sense of fashion, and nothing fit. I looked and felt terrible. The drill sergeant double-timed us to the buses, and we were lined up alphabetically by last name. My last name begins with a *G,* Tony and Billy were *A* and *C,* so we were separated. First day, and already I had lost my guys. If I'm not careful, I thought, I could start to cry. The bus trip to Dix was a blur. I dragged my ass to the barracks and tried to shut out the yelling and the horsing around. These yokels were having a good time. Parading around naked and snapping towels at each other. Figured if I got a hot shower and some sleep, the world would look brighter in the morning. I was checking around for a bunk to throw my stuff on when I was approached by a pimply faced hick with stripes on his arm. Held in place by a rubber band. A make-believe sergeant. He didn't say hello or ask my name. He just points and says, "Hey, private, grab a mop and clean this floor. Now." I really should have thought this through, you know, tried to play it cool. But no, I was like, "Who do you think you're talking to, punk? I am with the Halsey Bops, motherfucker. You mess with me, and I will kick your skinny, fucking ass." It was really funny, the first time all day I felt in control. He got this nervous tic, his lower lip quivered, and he couldn't look at me. The kid was scared shit. I smiled to myself, laid down and settled into a deep sleep.

I was still dozing and thought I was having a wet dream. Then, all of a sudden, I was soaking wet. Before I could figure out what was happening, I was in the air and stunned, fully awake when I hit the floor. Someone had drenched me with a pail of water, then tossed my bunk. My first reaction was, I'll kill the son of a bitch. But before I could open my eyes, the drill sergeant was all over me. No rubber bands holding his stripes. He was kicking the shit out of me with the brightest spit-shined boots I had ever seen. I tried to run, but he tackled me near the stairs, and I was airborne. Not like a paratrooper, but definitely in the air and headed down. The bastard had thrown me down the stairs, screaming something about my mother and faggots from Brooklyn. Lefty had told me to stay under the radar, not let them learn my name. Since they couldn't pronounce *Gioia,* I thought I would be OK. But now they knew my name, and they knew I was from Brooklyn. Fuckers would be able to find me by the sound of my voice.

Powder-Blue Pants

I've always had this thing about pants. Probably because I was a fat kid, weighing more than a hundred pounds before I reached double digits. Clothes just didn't fit right. Then Lefty gave me these powder-blue pants, and they fit. I still can't figure it out. I felt like I had just hit a grand slam in the bottom of the ninth. At 14 Holy Martyrs, we wore uniforms. Dark-blue pants, white shirt, and red tie through fourth grade. Then, when I was ten, we changed to a blue tie. The Catholic version of a fashion revolution.

Lefty was my favorite relative. My first cousin on my father's side. He was killer good looking, could shoot pool, and he drove a Caddy. He had an Irish girlfriend, Mary, with long red hair and even longer legs. In my family, they said things like "Clothes make the man." Looking good was important, and my father was one of the men who took it seriously. He was a sharp dresser. A Cesar Romero type. Whenever my mother suggested he wear his brown suit, he would say, "Brown is for old people like your father." Besides, her job was not to dress him but to see to it that his clothes were clean, pressed and hanging in the closet when he went to get dressed.

I had first seen Lefty wearing the pants on Christmas Eve. He wore them with a cobalt-blue shirt and a skinny, black, snakeskin belt. They had a three-inch rise, by which I mean that the belt loops were set down three inches from the top of the pants. The belt just asserted itself around his waist. It was probably when I first started to think about clothes. It was the Christmas I talked to him about seeing my Aunt Betty naked. The pants were an amazing shade of powder blue. A little like morpho butterflies in Costa Rica. They had a reverse pleat, a narrow cuff, probably less than an inch, and a twelve peg. Twelve isn't much, and you had to take your featherweights off to get the pants over your feet. When I was confirmed—the observance where you get to wear a red robe, like you've just graduated from college—Lefty, who was my godfather, gave me a Bulova watch that probably cost $50, and, because he knew I loved them, he gave me the pants too. I broke the crystal on the watch that first day, when it flew off my wrist throwing a pass to my kid brother in front of my grandfather's house on Gates Avenue. It was across the street from a private school, where the boys had really long sideburns and old men with long white beards made strange sounds while shaking their heads over large loaves of braided bread. The crystal could be replaced, but I really needed to take care of the pants. Since Lefty had given them to me, I wanted to show them off, wear them to school. True, they weren't dark blue, but they were in the same color family. We sat at wooden desks back then. The surface of your desk was somehow attached to the seat in front of you. Same as your seat was attached to the desk in back of you. They had a kind of art nouveau iron support on the sides that was screwed into the floor. Sometimes the screws came loose and the desk rocked a little. They were heavy, probably oak, and there was a shelf under the writing surface for your books and a cutout on the top to keep your pen and an inkwell. The inkwell was glass and had a brass cover. You lifted the cover and very carefully added ink straight from the bottle. I had a cheap, wine-red Waterman that I used to practice my cursive, to match the twenty-six letters of the alphabet posted around the room.

I won't get into how I got ink on the pants. It still hurts to think about it. I will tell you that the ink was blue-black and closely resembled the cobalt-blue shirt that Lefty wore. And when I took them to the dry cleaner, the woman I called Pearl, who wore a large zircon around her neck that I thought was a diamond, looked at the pants, shook her head and said, "Young fella, you go to that Catholic school around the corner, right? Because these pants, they need a little prayer and a lot of help. And just so you know, they don't have a snowball's chance in hell of coming clean."

Not Just the Good Old Boys

I joined the army on January 11, 1963. I needed to get out of the neighborhood for a while. Change my scene. The white horse was gaining on me, and I didn't know if I could outrun it. John had just OD'd, and I needed to leave those memories behind. It was a tough time, losing one of my closest guys. We had played stickball together since we were kids. Hung with the Halsey Bops in our teens and smoked grass together that first time. I had sworn I would never use, but I did. I had sworn I would never shoot, and didn't get that right either. I can still see him sitting on our stoop, lighting a Lucky and blowing smoke rings. His deep good looks framed by a perfectly combed pompadour and accented by a baby blue shirt that had the collar turned up. John was always ready for takeoff. Unfortunately, he never learned how to make a safe landing.

My basic training instructor at Fort Dix was Sergeant Doubles. They called him Doubles because he had only two fingers on one hand, the left. Korea. He thought I was a fuckup, and he didn't like my Brooklyn bravado, so he "volunteered" me a couple of times to let me know who was in charge. The time I remember most was the poison gas exercise. He made me and a few of the other wiseguys stand in a tent as he demonstrated how to put on a gas mask. When he finished, he said, "Now we'll see which of you men's been payin attention," and he dropped a canister of mustard gas on the ground. We had half a minute at most to get our gas masks on. "Three Mississippi, four Mississippi, five." In seconds my eyes started tearing and my face was on fire. I tried to hold my breath, but I couldn't stop coughing. We were bent over crying, some of us puking, when he let us outside and had one of the other recruits spray us with a hose. Then he yelled, "Smoke 'em if you've got 'em, faggots" and walked away laughing. "Fucking sadist." I had joined the army to learn a trade, get a good job when I got out. Meet a nice girl and get married . . . have kids. A normal life like a normal person. The recruiter handed me a book the size of a telephone directory. "Here, kid. Take a look at this. You can be anything you want." I went through it and selected teletypewriter repair. The coming of the computer age. They sent me to Fort Gordon in Augusta. Home of the Masters and the Signal Corps. Where white people lived on one side of the tracks and the ghetto was the other. Segregation. Where the black guys took me out to eat my first chicken sandwich. Bones and all between two pieces of Wonder Bread. When we left the chicken place, a car tried to run us down when we crossed the street together.

I wasn't very good at teletypewriter repair school and was told to report before a board of inquiry. An oversight board. There were three of them. Civilians. Good old boys. The chairman, wearing a red flannel shirt and smoking a cigar, spoke first. "Boy, we all hear you're not passing them there classes. Why is that, boy?" I explained that even though I worked hard at it, studied every night, I didn't have a very good aptitude for electronics. Then he said, "Where y'all from, boy?" "Brooklyn sir," I said. "Born and raised." He smiled and said, "Whatta y'all know, a city fella, and from Brooklyn, ya say. Don't that beat all. Whatta y'all good at, boy?" "I'm a really good cook," I told him, thinking I might be on to something. Then he turned to the guy next to him and said, "Charlie, whatta y'all think we should do with this here Brooklyn fella that cooks real good?" And Charlie crowed, "Well this here is Signal Corps, and cookin is Quartermaster Corps. No, sir, we gonna keep that boy right here in our own backyard. And if he can't learn ta fix the thingamajig, then I think we got us a real live infantry soldier here. You ever hearda Vietnam, boy? What say we give y'all a rifle and you can kill us some commie gooks? Would y'all like that, boy? Kill ya some commie gooks?"

Then, that's when I started to get scared.

Lessons from My Father

My father was not a nice man. When he died, my brothers and I listened to the mourners talk about what a terrific guy he was, how much he loved children. When I heard their lies, I screamed at them. My father was very good looking. A real sharpie. What they called a natty dresser. When he walked into a room, people noticed. He had a sense of mystery about him that attracted both men and women. Everyone wanted to be his friend, wanted Jerry to like them. People looked up to him, and it was easy for him to get his point across. He would just present whatever it was he was trying to make happen as reality. He would never ask if he could do something, just assumed he could. He was a truck driver and a small-time thief, but he talked his way into a successful real estate career, until they found out he had never gotten past grade school.

As I got older, I learned a certain arrogance from him, and inherited his confident swagger. My father was also a tough guy, so I wanted to be a tough guy too. In fact, he was a nasty son of a bitch, and it took me half a lifetime to understand that. He made his decisions based on whatever his needs might be. I knew he was a narcissist before I knew what the word meant. This is a small thing, but as a young boy I thought it was very exciting. If he needed a parking space, it didn't matter that another driver would already be backing in. He would just pull in from the other side and take the space. The guy would scream and frantically blow his horn. My father would roll down his window and yell, "Blow it out your ass." Then he would smile at me. What power!

As a kid, I heard the family whispers. Watched his eyes follow my aunt across the room. Was my father fucking my aunt? My father was fucking my aunt! I didn't see him much after he left us, didn't hear from him when I joined the army. Then, while I was in Vietnam, I got a letter with a fancy Five Towns return address. All friendly and light, like nothing had changed. "Dear Son," it said. "How are you? I've gotten married, and when you come home, I want you to meet my new wife." How am I? I thought. How the hell do you think I am? I'm in a fucking war, and I haven't heard from you since that day in the city. Your affair with Aunt Betty is over, and you've remarried. Am I supposed to give a shit? Apparently old money can provide more benefits than tits and ass that were now on the wrong side of forty. You tossed her aside just like you did my mother. Not that I cared about Aunt Betty anymore, but it reminded me how your world began and ended—to satisfy only you.

Then it all came flooding back. The day I had last seen you in New York. At Romeo's, a spaghetti joint on the "Deuce." In between bites of food camouflaged by red sauce, and indistinguishable from library paste, I had begged you to tell me why you left us when I was a kid. My drug use had become reckless, and I was long past being just a weekend warrior. I was eighteen, my life spiraling out of control, and I needed help. I wanted to move out of the city, maybe live with you. You were furious. "Are you crazy?" you said. "I've got enough complications in my life. Go home to your mother, leave me alone." I couldn't believe what I was hearing. This was the same man who had taken me to his uncle's restaurant to show me off to his friends. Fed me roasted lamb brains from the end of his fork. "But you're my dad," I said, and you looked at me and said, "Not anymore, Frankie. Not anymore." Was it true? You no longer loved me? Did you know, it's been almost sixty years, and I've never gotten over it? I still remember the tears streaming down my face as I walked down Eight Avenue to Thirty-Fourth Street. Descended the stairs into the subway and caught the local back to Brooklyn.

The Library

So Rocky shoves a large brown paper bag across the table, and I open it to look inside. Wait, hang on a second, I'm getting ahead of myself here. I'm home, sleeping. It's like eight in the morning and Rocky calls me. "What are you doing?" he says. "What the fuck do you think I'm doing? It's eight o'clock. I was sleeping." "We need to talk," he tells me. "Meet me at Tony's right away." The coffee shop on Central. It's where he hangs out when he's not in the poolroom or at the track. Tony's is a daytime destination for coffee and ham and egg sandwiches. Bookies and grave diggers starting the day, hookers ending theirs.

We sit at a small, white Formica table, away from the ten red vinyl stools facing the counter, and away from Tony, who stands at the stove like a priest at the altar. Rocky puts a large paper bag in front of me. "Check it out," he says, his face a riot of smiles. He's ripped off Farrell's pharmacy. Broke in during the night. "Child's play," he adds. "Like money in the bank." Knocked out the bulb in the alley, pried open the window with a screwdriver. Took everything he could stuff in the bag, in and out in less than five minutes. He's been trying to figure out what he has all morning. I mean, you can't just shoot the shit without having at least some idea what it is. We need to do some research. Due diligence.

At ten, we head out to the library. Since neither of us drives a car, we have to take the train. The elevated line on Chauncey, then change at Eastern Parkway for the local to Jamaica. It's 1959, and where they have colored women to clean the houses, that's where they have libraries. We sit at one end of a large oak table. One by one we remove a bottle from the bag, read the label, and see if we can find it in the PDR. Soon we have three little piles. The good stuff now consists of Dilaudid, codeine, and belladonna. The maybe pile, which you might use if you were strung out, and the stuff we need to flush down the toilet.

We take the bag and head out to Rock's pad on Bushwick. He needs to shoot. What was a chippie is now a habit, and he needs to shoot at least once every day. Rocky is older, late twenties, and has his own apartment. He's the guy who turned me on to grass. And smack too. Backed me whenever I played three-cushion billiards. He also introduced me to opera and jazz. In my house, they only listened to music that could pass the ethnicity test. Singers like Tony Bennett and Perry Como. Here, I am mesmerized by this music without words. The place is fully furnished, brocade hanging from the windows, doilies on the chairs. Like some old grandmother's place. I don't get it until some weeks later, when Paulie starts to sleep over and they don't mess up the second bed.

We lay out the haul on the dining room table. Re-create the three little piles. John and Eugene join us, and Rocky gets his works. Works consist of an eyedropper, a stainless steel needle, and an aspirin bottle cap fastened with a piece of wire to hold the fix. A book of matches to cook, and it all fits inside a Marlboro box. We add a few drops of water and a small piece of cotton, the backing off a button from an Ivy League shirt to absorb the shot. I watch the heated powder become liquid, and my hands get clammy. Rock takes off his belt to tie up, and we're all set. Beginners like me only skin-pop, so I pass on the belt. Talk on the street is that you can't get a habit if you don't shoot the vein. We try the Dilaudid first, but it's tricky to figure out how much to take. It's not like you get directions when you cop a bag of H, but you learn by how high you get, whether two or even three guys can share a $5 bag. Lester Young provides the soundtrack. We spend the afternoon nodding to his horn.

The Poolroom

I heard him yell as soon as I walked in the door. "Hey, fatboy! Whatthefuckareyoudoinhere? Letsseeyourfuckinpapers." The long, narrow room was painted puke green. The six windows along the avenue were black. The jukebox was blasting Sinatra's "You Make Me Feel So Young" as the smoke from my Lucky Strike drifted into the dusty glare. You can do this, I told myself. You just need to prove you're sixteen. You've got papers, for Chrissake. A baptismal certificate with a seal from the church. He can't argue with the church. Last night we had shown up at the rectory during the priest's dinner hour. Acting as the front, I humbly explained that we needed to talk with the pastor about a very troubling matter. The maid, wrinkled by years of caring for these princes of the church, escorted us inside and had us wait in the holy father's study. The safe was unlocked, and we were in business. Besides, no one would question us. We were graduates of 14 Holy Martyrs. Class of '56. Tony, built like a jockey, crawled inside the safe to search for the blank forms. John, with nerves of steel, removed the metal die from its velvet box and stamped it with the official seal. Outside, I leaned over the hood of an old Buick and used my Catholic-school handwriting to forge the pastor's signature.

I tried not to look at Nufi when I handed him the fake baptismal. Standing in front of the Kim Novak calendar and putting on my best "I'm cool" face, I checked out the scene. At the king table up front, four guys were playing money ball. Nine Ball Blackie was hustling some kid on table two, and then came a billiard table. It had no pockets and only three balls. Two white, one red. At the four tables in the rear, an assortment of hustlers and pretty boys circled each other like hawks smelling blood. Industrial metal lights hung above each table. Black and white wooden beads, suspended on metal wires and reachable only with the tip of a pool cue, were used to track the score. I tried to relax, but my entire body was locked in place. Like the first time I kissed Rosemary Spumonti. Man, what lips! She could swallow you whole. By this time, Nufi was reciting the rules of the house, but I didn't hear a fucking word. I was in, baby. I would be fifteen in two weeks.

The sounds of the poolroom brought me back to the moment. "*Your rack. Listen to me. I'm telling you, he's turkey. You spot him 65–50 and still take his bread. Believe it, she's cherry. Can't you see the way she walks? Four ball, side pocket. Thirteen in the corner. You talking about my sister? No? You better not be, Paddy Boy, or I will kick your fucking ass. Didja hear? Who won the second at Belmont? I hit the first. Little Augie by a neck. Went off at sixteen to one. A lock. Paid $34.60. If I hit the double, I'm buying Hollywood mufflers for my Chevy. Seven, cross side. Five in the corner. He did. Paid me $5 once to shit on his hands.*"

A couple of weeks later, I was shooting on the billiards table when an older, good-looking guy approached me. "Hi," he said. "I'm Joey. You play?" Joe Z. was legend in Brooklyn. A local gambler and a pool shark, his soft-spoken proposal was dripping. A ten-point game. Even up. No spot or handicap given to either player. A little wager to make it interesting. He suggested $50. My wallet held $25, but I had never bet more than $10 in my life. I guess that was the point. He expected me to be nervous, and I was. What he didn't know was that my friend Rocky had been teaching me how to play billiards, and I was good at it. After a round of bullshitting back and forth, he agreed to spot me two points. I would need to make eight to his ten. I put down my $25, and Rock covered the rest. He won the lag, got to shoot first, and made the opening shot. In no time, I was down two, zip. So I took Rock's advice and shot a hanger if there was one or played him safe. It soon became clear that my understanding of this arcane game was better than his. He began to lose it when it became 6–5 in my favor. I reached eight before he did, and he was thoroughly pissed. Up $25, it was an easy call agreeing to his suggestion that we shoot spot shots for $10 a shot. We were now playing with his money, and I was feeling very confident. Twenty minutes later, his last $30 was mine. A major score. I won

$55. I walked over to Vincent's tailor shop on Decatur Street and was fitted for two custom-made pairs of pants. Twenty-five dollars a pop. A three-inch rise, twelve peg, pleats, and slash pockets. One black sharkskin, the other iridescent green.

And They're Off

Louie, who we used to call No-Back because he couldn't pronounce Kim Novak, played the ponies in his free time and loved to talk about horse racing whenever some of the guys were around. He was a grave digger at Evergreen Cemetery, and you could find him most mornings at Tony's coffee shop, handicapping the day's races at Belmont and Aqueduct, or Santa Anita during winter, when the New York tracks were closed. Louie was drawn to celebrity and loved to talk about the day in '49 when he dug the grave for Luther Robinson, or as Louie would say, Lutha. Mr. Robinson, also known as Bojangles, was a hoofer from the thirties who had danced in Hollywood films with Shirley Temple.

From my mornings hanging out in the coffee shop, waiting for the poolroom to open, I learned that most gamblers, including horse players, have an unyielding faith in their ability to beat the odds. They would purchase the *Racing Form* every morning and spend the time before work going over the past histories of horses, jockeys, and trainers for any clues they thought would give them an edge. Picking winners is complicated, and that is why in the old days, when bookies covered the bets, they usually had the nicest cars around. A fact that probably led the states to go into the gambling business.

No-Back and Rocky loved to talk about horse racing, and they developed an ongoing rivalry around who was the better handicapper. Of course, it wasn't just confined to the two of them. A number of other guys also chimed in. There was the day Rock hit a fifty-to-one shot and couldn't resist letting Louie know about it. "Hey, Lou, didja hear? I hit the fifth at Belmont. Independence Day. Paid $102.40. A cakewalk," he told him with a big smile. "C'mon, sit down, I'll buy you a coffee. How about a Danish?" "Thanks," said Louie somewhat sarcastically. "So whattaya want, a marching band, we should shoot off fireworks or somethin?" "Just wished I had 'em across the board, that's all," replied Rocky wistfully. Nine Ball Blackie, who was sitting across the way with Batty—the Bat Man they called him—says so everyone can hear, "Listen ta this, willya? Last week I got a tip from that tout over at Josie's Bar, you know, what's his name? Anyway, he sez ta me, I should watch this horse, Polly Wants a Cracker, the next time out. He's ready ta graduate," he says. "Especially if it's rainin. The horse is a mudder, and it rained all fuckin day last Wednesday. Out of the gate like a bat out of hell." He laughs and says, "Bat outta hell, that's a good one, huh, Batty?" "Fuck you, Blackie," says Batty. "Ya know what I'm sayin?"

Now Louie starts to laugh, and he says, "Fuck that Danish, too sweet, and I'm watching my weight. Tony, let me have a ham and egg on a hard roll. Were you at the track yesterday?" he asks Rocky. "No, you bet with the book? The bagman been around yet to settle up? I was there with Crazy Legs. Had Ladybug in the first and Buried Treasure in the second. Ta win and ta show. Ya know the way he always bets just ta show? Takes his payday, and tomorrow can wait. So anyway, I've got a twin sawbuck ridin on the daily double. This Ladybug, a filly, breaks out of the gate like a rabbit. Really on the bit. The trainers been blowin her out, saw it in the morning's sheet, and she is so ready. A half mile in like 0:46 and six furlongs in 1:10. Never flattened out, fully extended, wire to wire. But this Buried Treasure is another story." "You had him too?" yells Fat Jimmy Biangolina, the Bleach Man. Jimmy was Batty's older brother and did very well in the old neighborhood. All those Italian ladies were convinced that cleanliness was next to godliness, so Jimmy's bleach was used religiously. And because the gallons were so heavy, he always had some young, strong guys willing to run up to the third or fourth floor for ten bucks a day. So the old ladies didn't have to come down, take them away from watching *General Hospital* or *Guiding Light*. "I seen him in the paddock," Jimmy says, "with blinders on, and I started ta get nervous. Where was you?" "I was on the rail," says Louie, "in the homestretch, near the finish line. I always stand close ta the wire. In case it's a photo finish. Gives me a good angle so I can see if the nag is leavin it all out there or just airin it out." "Anyway," says Jimmy, "he's gotta be able to keep his focus, not bolt on me. Plus it's a baby race, and if he gets boxed in, I'm fucked. He broke good though, right, Lou? Layin off the pace? It's only five and a half furlongs, and the Shoe is riding him. At the sixteenth pole, Shoemaker taps him once with the bat, with those velvety hands of his, and this Buried Treasure turns into a regular Silky Sullivan. Makes up probably ten lengths and wins goin away. Like the rest of them was standing still. But you had the double? Madon! You musta won a bundle." "Yeah, I did alright," says No-Back, and he starts to sing "I'm as rich as Rockefeller," a line from "On the Sunny Side of the Street," and he got up from the table and did a little soft-shoe out the door.

First Impressions

The long line of wrinkled khaki moved slowly forward. Pasty-faced farm boys and tough guys with vacant eyes, newly minted lieutenants and lifers who had been there. A stewardess hugged me as we left the plane, and I felt exposed. She had read the fear in my eyes, and it reminded me not to get into any poker games. Outside, on the open air bridge, I was smacked by heat so intense that not even riding the IND line in summer had prepared me for it. We fried on the seething tarmac while the roar of aircraft engines and the frenetic swirling of helicopter gunships mingled with the acrid smell of burning fuel. Tan Son Nhut Air Base, October 1963. I grabbed a seat on the army bus and tried to calm down, breaking into laughter as a platoon of ARVN troops passed by holding hands. It would be okay. I would only be here for a year. Guys from the block had done more time for doing a little dealing. Piece of cake, I thought, but who was I bullshitting?

The bus dropped me at battalion supply, where I was issued combat boots, a steel helmet, and an M1 rifle. My ass was dragging. I would have killed for a shower. My mouth felt like someone had pushed my face in the sand at Rockaway, and sweat poured from my newly muscled body. Previously a chubby guy, I was now a middleweight. Thanks to Army basic and food so bad that fasting was often the best alternative. I was napping, dreaming of undressing the winning contestant in the Miss America pageant, when the wailing sirens stunned me awake. It was still daytime, and through the screened walls of the barracks, I watched young boys posing as men, rifles in hand, scattering in all directions. Still groggy, I was fully awakened by the screaming of a private sent to find all the stragglers to report for duty. Grabbing my weapon, I ran to my post.

My stomach churning, I stared wide-eyed and terrified as four T-28 bombers maneuvered like silver birds in the blue sky and took turns swooping down out of the clouds to drop their ordnance. Like circus acrobats, they returned safely ahead of the puffy white imprint of the antiaircraft fire to await their next turn up. Fortunately, we were not the target. The bombing was directed at the palace of President Diem and his sister, Madame Nhu. The Kennedys had grown tired of Saigon's feeble efforts against the Viet Cong, and these precision flyers worked for the CIA. It was time for a change, and we had made a trade. Minh and Thieu would be the major players on our new team.

A heated exchange caught my attention, and I watched as an Asian noncom argued with a sergeant major. Although only a staff sergeant, he would not back down. He was making the point that we, his men, were technicians first, then soldiers, and there was no fucking way he was going to get us killed playing GI Joe. Eventually, we were ordered back to the barracks. In the future, we would only be issued our rifles if he said so. My heart skipped a beat. Who was this savior? Sergeant Kane turned out to be a lifer from Maui who had chosen the army over poverty after doing two tours in World War II. He had served almost twenty years and wouldn't see another stripe unless he could change his pigment from yellow to white. Under the parachute-shaded hooch, somebody broke out a bottle of Johnny Walker. Clean glasses appeared, and we began to tell our stories. Randle, clean and white, from the Midwest. Joined to protect our Christian country from communism. Wife and two kids back home. Yoshi, tough guy from Samoa. Drafted at twenty. Would be returning home next month and carried his swagger stick to prove it. Lynch, black kid from Newark. "Do time for boosting that car or serve your country," said the man sitting up high in the flowing midnight robe. Schmidt, pimply-faced drunk with six years of service and only one lonely stripe to show for it. Me? The street life had seduced me, and I needed to get out of the neighborhood for a while.

In walked Russo, lugging a care package from his politically connected family in Rhode Island. Never gave a thought to not doing his duty for God and country. Besides, it would look good on his resume if he decided to run for Congress. The first whiff was heaven. Aged provolone that would make your gums itch and dried sausage to marry it with. Marinated mushrooms, roasted peppers, and olives. Panettone and biscotti for dessert. And Russo, drenched with the generosity of his immigrant parents, sharing it all. Hey, somebody pass the whiskey.

Say It Isn't So

I met Jackie through my man Billie when he took me to her place on my twenty-first birthday. Jackie was a prostitute and a sexual seeker. An exciting older woman, probably twice my age, with a great body. Soon, she became my teacher. It was one of the few times that I enjoyed taking lessons. You entered her room through the rear of a local bar in downtown Saigon, where we often stopped for a Ba Muoi Ba, or 33 for short, the local formaldehyde-preserved brew. The door led to a courtyard off a public alley. She had dolled up the room to look like Versailles. Dark and quiet, with white sheets of pure silk. Of course, you still had to hit the alley whenever you needed to take a piss, or squat over a hole to take a shit. Inside the room, though, it was pure bliss, and we spent a number of memorable hours just hanging out. She liked me and I liked her, and she taught me how to experience pleasure in ways I had previously only fantasized about. I had gone to Catholic school and didn't have much sexual experience when I joined the army. Before Jackie, the sexual content running around in my brain was mostly what the church called impure thoughts. Hanging out with virgins believing in Jesus will do that to you. Being a prostitute in wartime was a competitive business, and Jackie charged very little for her services. She was very generous with me, and we got together often without dealing in the business end of things. She also turned me on to opium, and we spent a number of dazed afternoons passing a pipe back and forth.

One Sunday I was sitting in the bar waiting to see her and was approached by the bartender, a beautiful young woman with a great smile. Kind of like the girl next door, Vietnamese-style. It turned out that Jackie was away for the day, and I needed to come up with another plan. Rosie suggested we spend some time together, as her shift was almost over and she would love to hear about life in America. A drink and a short cab ride later, we were in a small room with cardboard walls, squeezed into a single bed that rested on a dirt floor. I tried to give her a few dollars, but she adamantly refused. It turned out that Rosie was not a working girl. She was hoping to marry a GI and get to the States. She spent the afternoon telling me what a good wife she would be and how she would make beautiful babies. How she liked to fuck-fuck. She introduced me to her parents, and her mother cooked me a meal. It was definitely a family affair. I was amused and, I have to admit, somewhat flattered by all the attention, but I was looking for an afternoon's dalliance, not to get married.

Two weeks later, I entered the bar on a Saturday afternoon, intent on seeing Jackie. I had just gotten paid and planned on spending the cocktail hour in a state of sexual ecstasy. Rosie was working and beamed when she saw me, thinking I was there to see her. This created some confusion, but since I hadn't made any promises and had been straight with her, even told her about my girl back home, I assumed it wouldn't be a problem. The bar was quiet, but when Rosie realized I was there to see Jackie, she started to yell. When she picked up the cleaver used to break up the ice for drinks, I bolted for the alley and what I hoped would be safety in Jackie's room. Unfortunately, she was with another client, and Rosie followed, screaming that she was going to cut my balls off. I tried pleading my case, but soon a crowd gathered. While the women argued, the men just smoked their black-market Chesterfields and smiled against the background roar of Anglo-Vietnamese. In minutes, this ad hoc court determined that I was guilty of having tarnished Rosie's reputation. If I didn't promise to marry her, the women said, she should use the cleaver to cut my thing off. Seeing no other way out, I smiled my best smile, told her I loved her, promised to get married, and got the fuck out of there as quickly as I could. Needless to say, I never went back to see Jackie again. Such a shame. I had so much more to learn.

Hamilton, the Original

For a while there, *Hamilton* was the hottest ticket on Broadway. With all due respect to the playwright, Lin-Manuel Miranda, I embraced Hamilton long before he did. It was 1956, and following the lead of my guys, I attended Alexander Hamilton Vocational High School so I could learn a trade. College not yet discovered in our corner of Brooklyn. I remember making a really cool dustpan once; another time, a ball-peen hammer. The days when manufacturing was king. The school was at Kingston and Throop in Bed-Stuy, a ghetto years before Bushwick. The three of us—me, John, and Tony—would meet at Bondy's candy store before eight. Teddy, the owner, would be putting out the papers. Wanting to talk baseball. I remind him that I need to get my ass in gear. Set off on our journey into the underground. We take the local on Wilson and converge with hundreds of screaming teenagers at Eastern Parkway. Scattering into the tunnels of our choice. Our destinations determined by the grade school we had attended and the amount of money our parents had. The screeching of the trains and the screams of the marauding hordes clashing with the sober looks of the desk jockeys as they considered the racing form in the morning tabloids.

I had come from a good Catholic grammar school. Made my First Communion and was confirmed in the shadow of its church's spires. When it was time to graduate, I almost didn't get my diploma. I had missed the mandatory nine o'clock Mass, and the penguin in charge, Sister Donna Marie, questioned my Catholic belief. When I couldn't remember the sermon read at the later Mass I attended, she threatened to keep me from graduating. My mom had spent ten bucks to rent the cap and gown, and there was no fucking way I wouldn't get to wear it. I snuck into class before the three o'clock ceremony, ripped open the box of certificates and took mine. The Archdiocese of Brooklyn hereby awards its highest honor to Frank Nicholas Gioia.

At our stop, we were greeted by hookers with their skirts hiked up to here. Does she even have panties on? Winos in the doorways of the long-ago-closed stores. The windows covered in ripped and faded paper signs shouting 75% OFF. EVERYTHING MUST GO. We stopped for cigarettes at the same hole-in-the-wall, to buy loosies every morning. Two for a nickel and the three of us shared them. That's the way it was with my guys. We took care of each other. We had learned it at an early age, when family was traded for friendship. Some of our fathers having moved on to other bedrooms.

The school was a large brick behemoth occupying an entire square block. Doo-wop, the dominant sound, drifting through the ancient hallways. Black kids, members of the Chaplains and the Bishops, and white boys doing their best bopping imitations. Assembly every Wednesday, with a show equal to anything you could see at the Brooklyn Paramount. Louie Lymon, Frankie's brother, he of "Why Do Fools Fall in Love" fame, was the big name. Louie sang lead with the Teenchords. Dressed in their striped suits and skinny ties, they rocked the Hamilton stage. It was my first exposure to black people not filtered through newspapers and TV. Turned out we weren't that different, just a bunch of guys trying to prove who had the best moves. Looking to score on the basketball court, and hoping to score with their girlfriends.

That summer we spent nearly every Friday night in Putnam Park, listening to white guys trying to sound black as they harmonized for the weekly Battle of the Groups. Tony and the Fascinators, guys from the neighborhood singing "Chapel Bells." Watching in awe as the song climbed the charts. Convinced that an Italian greaser would become a star. By then, the Halsey Bops had taken over Halsey Park, the old men like my grandfather having passed on to that big amusement park in the sky. In Bushwick we joined with the Ellery Bops, and together we controlled the streets from Evergreen Cemetery to East New York. Where a year or so later, me and Rocky would catch the bus in front of Red's bakery to the foot of the Williamsburg Bridge to score. Cooking fairy dust and shooting up in the basements of boarded-up buildings. Now my friends' children, newly married, pay $2,500 a month to live in a studio apartment the size of a closet. Can two people even fit in a closet?

The Mercury Man

We were playing stickball, dodging the cars and buses as usual, just down the block from my house. My father wasn't working, so it must have been a Saturday. Until then, the only car I had ever seen him drive was our '49 Buick. That day he drove down Schaefer in a new, 1954 blue Mercury. Just out of the showroom. The chrome bullets on the front bumper shimmered in the afternoon light. Like the car was alive. Parked it in front of our house. When he opened the driver's-side door, the smirk on his face told the whole story. That "I just know I'm going to get that piece of ass" look spread across his face. Naturally, I thought the car was ours, mine. Didn't know my father had other plans. That even though the car was new, he was closing an old chapter in his life. Our lives. In a few months he would point the car east toward Long Island, toward Aunt Betty's. Never look back. He lived there the rest of his life. Probably one of the reasons I never did.

My mother, who loved the Buick, didn't like the Mercury. Was pissed that my father spent over two grand on a car without talking to her about it. Maybe she saw the bigger picture. What I see when I close my eyes is them fighting in the hall. It's too painful to watch, and my eyes stay glued to the shit-brown, fake wainscoting. I stare at it so I don't have to look at them. I can still hear them yelling. I can't shut them out. My mother saying, "You're a good-for-nothing bum. Do you hear me? You're a *puttana* Jerry, a whore. I should have listened to my papa. Never married you." She holds on to the car's keys, swings her arms wildly while blocking the frosted-glass door to the outside. My father raises his hands to defend himself as her punches rain down on him. I worry that the glass will break and she will get hurt. I beg them, "Please, please don't fight," but they're not listening. I can still see the look on his face, that he had found himself in this situation. Calling her a crazy bitch, just wanting to get out of the house as quickly as possible. To leave this mess he had created in the rearview mirror.

"Never, ever use his name in this house again." My mother screamed it at us, said it over and over whenever she needed to vent her anger, feel her pain. She called my father the "Mercury Man." It became his new name, beginning on the day he left us. She never referred to him as "your father" again. Never acknowledged his existence, although she kept his last name. Maybe it was her way of holding on to the past, not having to embrace this new reality. But why? This is the same man whose running around tortured her. She cried over the lipstick on his collar, kept his cum-stained pants hanging in the closet. His new life absorbed her every waking moment. She was devastated that he had left her with three children, hated him for what he had done. Sometimes, when we upset her, she took it out on us. Crying and chasing me and my brothers around the house, desperately swinging a handful of leather belts. Stopping only when her sobbing made it impossible to continue.

My father became the Mercury Man, and I became the man of the house. Not yet twelve and being told I was a man. That I was now responsible for taking care of my mother, my younger brothers. This was new territory, something my aunts and uncles dreamed up. Some of the same relatives I would never see again, because of my parents divorce. People took sides, the family was broken. Compound fractures, they never healed.

At school, the church pastor sought me out to talk about the family's problems. Tried to convince me to join God's team, become a priest. It was a lot to think about. First off, I would need to learn Latin. Take my Catholicism much more seriously, go to church on Sundays. Never have sex. Really? Never have sex? I was just learning the rules of the game. Now he wanted me to play for another team. Fuck that, I thought. I like my team, and before I think about switching sides, I at least want a chance to give it a try.

Craps

He threw down a few crumpled bills near the brick wall. Someone standing in the crowd said, "You're covered, man. Go ahead . . . roll 'em." The shooter blew into his fist, shook his right hand, closed his eyes, and said to himself, as if in prayer: "Help me, Jesus. Bless me, Mary and Joseph. Show me a seven, baby, seven." Then this other guy said, "Throw the fucking bones already, willya? Snake eyes, baby, snake eyes." I listened as the sounds from the dice game drifted over to the wooden benches. The lingo of craps was familiar to me. I had watched Lefty and his friends play outside Sal's pool hall on Madison. You only needed a wall—a garage door would do—and a few guys feeling lucky, a little money in their pockets.

I hadn't played before, not for real money. This was for dollars, not some loose change. Up until then, my experience with dice had been playing Monopoly. But I was itching to give it a try. The worst I could do was lose a few bucks. You had to know when to lay your money down, when not to. Bet strategic. It was all about the shooter. He controlled the dice and the betting. Sure, luck was part of it, but skill entered into it too. Was the shooter hot or cold? What point did he need to hit to win? You had a better chance of throwing a six or an eight than the odds of hitting an outside number like a four or a five, or a nine and ten.

We were hanging outside the garages, near the poolroom, around the corner from Jimmy's apartment on Central. It was where he kept his '56 Lincoln. Shiny black, with suicide doors. I was hanging back, watching the action. The shooter was hot, had thrown a natural on two of his first three rolls. Had hit a tough point, Little Joe, a four, in between. Throw a seven or eleven, a natural on the initial roll, and you're a winner. Throw a seven after the point has been established, and you lose. The point is the number you have to match if you don't throw a natural on the first roll. Now the shooter had a fistfull of dollars in his left hand, the cubes in his right. He laid down a ten-spot, and a couple of guys took five each to cover. Little Louie bet a pound on a fade and started yelling, "C'mon, Mama, boxcars. Craps for daddy." A fade is a side bet, either for or against the shooter. The guy said, "Seven eleven, baby, seven eleven," and let the dice fly. "Boxcars, mother fucker, boxcars." The sounds of the players told you all you needed to know. The shooter started cursing because he had let the winning bets ride, played double or nothing. So when he rolled craps, he lost everything. Craps is either a two, snake eyes, a three or a twelve, boxcars, on the first roll. Throw any of those before the point is set, and you lose. Throw it after, and it doesn't mean shit. One of the older guys said, "Who's up?" If I wanted in, it was my roll. I picked up the dice and felt my belly tighten. I threw down a deuce, and somebody snickered and said, "I've got the heavy hitter. You're covered, big guy. Roll 'em." I shook my right hand and heard myself say, "Let er rip. C'mon seven," and I let them fly. They came up eleven, and I was up two bucks. "Let it ride," I said, and I could feel myself start to relax. The shooter controls the ivories for as long as he keeps winning. "Baby needs a new pair of shoes," I shouted, and won again with a seven. "Fuck this shit! First a natural, now the devil," the guy who covered my bets said. The tone of his voice betraying how pissed off he was. Now I'm up six bucks, and I didn't know what the bones could still give me. So I said, "Take it down," and picked up half the eight singles lying on the ground. I rolled the dice and threw craps, a three, and Louie started yelling, "Acey, deucey, Mama. Acey, deucey. My roll."

Jimmy shouted down from the kitchen window, "Hey, Frankie, wanna go for a ride?" "Sure," I said. "I'm up a deuce, man. I'll buy you an ice cream."

Poker Face

Me and Jimmy head over to Bondy's, on Wilson, to grab a couple of cones. Mary's working the counter, so I straddle a stool and stand up so I can get a better look. I stare, licking my lips, watching her bend over the freezer with the ice cream scoop. Savoring the view of her big-girl tits bursting from her too-small black bra. Smiling as her breasts make an entrance. I think about the first time I saw them. The tattoo on her left breast. An *A* and then some numbers, a math I don't understand. When she straightens up, she smiles like she knows I'm looking at her and doesn't care. Maybe even likes it. I get vanilla on a sugar cone; Jimmy gets chocolate, plain cone, both with sprinkles. I lay a quarter on the counter, and we slide into a booth to enjoy the moment. "Man, she's got great tits," he says. "I know, tell me about it," I laugh. Then her husband, Teddy—he's got the numbers on his left forearm—comes over to say hello. "You boys see Furillo last night? Threw out what's-his-name, Dark, Alvin Dark, the shortstop for the Giants. He tried to score from second on a double. Off the wall in right. An arm like a cannon, that one. A good Wop arm, excuse please, an Italian arm, from right here in Brooklyn. The Dodgers. You boys see it on the TV? Did you?"

He sounds pretty excited, talking baseball. America's game. Me, I'm thinking of Mary's tits, the numbers. We finish our cones and get back in the car. Jimmy revs the Lincoln, peels out, and burns rubber halfway down the street. He parks in front of my house. My brother Joe and some of the guys are hanging out on the stoop. It's the place where we first played one of our countless ball games, throwing a pink rubber Spalding against the steps. Now it's where we meet to grab a smoke, try to look cool. They are playing cards. My brother shuffles, executes a bridge that whistles, and passes the cards to his left, asks Little Paulie to cut. "Dealer's choice," he says. "Seven-card stud, one-eyed jacks wild. Ante up." The pot holds fifty cents. He deals each player three down cards, says "roll your own," and they select a card to turn up. They are hunched over like question marks, studying the cards, hoping and praying, while my brother controls the deck. "First king bets," he tells them, and deals another card. "Pair of kings, a four to the five, a deuce to the trey, and another king. Dealer draws a ten. Check it out, baby, a pair of dimes." Let the posing begin. The role fits him like a new pair of dress socks. A couple of guys fold, and he deals another card. "A nickel to the kings, no help for the cowboys this round. Another five, pair of fives, and an ace for my tens. Still kings' bet." "Kings bet a quarter," Little Paulie says, trying to force his hand. "Bump you a quarter," says my brother, and you can feel the shift. Will they never learn? Paulie probably has two pair. My brother would need aces over to beat his kings. Before and after the last down card, there are betting rounds. Joe raises both times. Paulie calls the bets, but you can read it on his face. It's slipping away. "Whatta ya got?" asks the dealer. "Kings over," Paulie says, and my brother reaches for the pot as he turns over the one-eyed jack of spades. His last down card. Three tens. Paulie had tens in the hole, thought maybe he had a chance. Hoping against hope. It's hard to admit sometimes, because my brother is younger, but he's the best fucking cardplayer on the block. A shark. Nobody even comes close. I mean, he could be down a fin, and you wouldn't know it. His affect never changes. Plus, he's a lucky son of a bitch. I take a seat, but not to play, just to sit and watch. To wait for the time when he gives me the signal to start the routine we run when it's time to pick up the winnings. Count the change. In the meantime, I'm thinking of Mary and the numbers, and I watch as two buzzards circle ominously overhead. Diving toward the pigeon coop on the six-family across the street. Then pulling up at the last second as the pigeons scream, and the hawks have to turn away from the barrier of the coop. Then diving again and repeating the process multiple times as the afternoon wears on and the pile of nickels, dimes, and quarters in front of my brother grows larger. It's getting near five when he lifts his chin, raises his eyes. Just a little, almost imperceptibly. Slowly

I get up, stretch towards the sky. Watch the birds do a final dive and head inside to tell my mom. She's looking in the refrigerator, surveying the leftovers. "He's up at least ten bucks, probably more," I say. She gets a serene look, goes to the door and yells, "Joe, it's time to eat. Make this the last hand." All the losers groan. "Fuck, man, you can't just quit when you're ahead." "Like hell I can't," he says. "Gotta eat. Hey, don't worry. Tomorrow's another day."

He drops the change on the kitchen table, laughs as he groups it into piles. "You were there when I bluffed Paulie, right? I was showing a pair of dimes, and he had the other two tens. Thought he was home free. As soon as I upped the bet, you could see his face drop. Folded like a tent in the wind. Nice guy, but he's no Maverick. Shit, even God doesn't play dice with the universe." There are five or six stacks, mostly quarters, plus a little loose change left over. "Here Ma," he says, and points to the piles on the table, puts a few nickels and dimes in his pocket. She picks up the money, drops the coins into her now pregnant change purse, hugs him, and radiates a hundred-watt smile. Then she digs out two crumpled one-dollar bills from inside her black plastic handbag. "Frankie, go to the corner and get some cutlets. From Dimmy, the butcher. A pound. Make sure he cuts them thin, the way I like them." I run into Little Paulie on the way. He was the big loser, and he's pissed. "Always gotta go in, your brother, as soon as he starts winning. What's up with that? I mean, what the fuck?" Paulie's one of my people, so I let him shoot his mouth for a few. Blow off some steam. We're friends, but, hey, it's my brother we're talking about here, so it's not like I'm shedding any tears. Besides, no one twisted his arm. He chose to jump in the tank, nobody threw him in. You wanna swim with the sharks, you gotta expect some blood.

Giuseppe

They had dressed him in a dark blue suit, starched white shirt, black tie, black socks and shoes. His hair, silvery white. Still wavy like mine. Clean shave, manicured nails, and trimmed mustache. Impeccable. Lying flat, hands folded, holding the rosary over his groin. The door opens. Someone yells, "Get two," and the sounds of the schoolyard seep into the funeral home. Corso's is directly across the street from PS 106. I'm thinking about the game as Pasquale shuffles into the stillness of the chapel. He is dressed all in black, his eyes, red and puffy. His best friend, my grandfather, Giuseppe Giarraputo, eighty-four years old, has died. I'm still just a kid, the person chosen to represent the family while the adults are working.

I didn't ask for this job. I don't want this fucking job. I'm not really comfortable around the dead. I knew it the first time, when they took us to Mary Anne's funeral. She was eight. I was in first grade. Something with her heart. The wake in the second-floor apartment, she dressed in white, laid out for viewing like a saint. All the little Catholic schoolchildren filing past. You could smell the corned beef from the kitchen. I thought I would puke. Besides, I don't speak the dialect, and my grandfather's friends don't speak much English. Pasquale offers his hand and his condolences. We make do with an assortment of grunts and gestures. He extends his cane and very slowly walks to the coffin. He says a prayer, struggles back to my side, hands me three one-dollar bills, and leaves.

I get up to mark the three dollars in the register, and I think I might faint. I open the door to breathe. Memories flood my brain. He called me a bum again last month because I went to the poolroom. I heard him tell my mom, "I'm a tella you, Rosa, he's a gonna be a bumma. Poola room. Notta good for a younga boy." He smoked cigars; dry, black leaf. Guinea stinkers. First thing in the morning with his breakfast. An off-white, chipped bowl, filled with coffee, milk, whiskey, and a raw egg. Can't forget to mark the register. It's important, so when Pasquale dies, my family will know how much to give his family. Records were kept for all events. Weddings, First Communions, births, and deaths. It feels tribal, and I like it. In the same vein as an eye for an eye.

I am now feeling both nauseous and anxious. It reminds me of the day they took me to the chicken market. I must have been six or seven. Linden Street, still Bushwick, but closer to the city. More Italian, less Irish. It's probably why my grandfather came, in case we ran into anyone from the Old Country. It's where we always went to buy fresh pasta, pastries, tomatoes by the case. A square, red brick building with a cement floor. A large garage door to one side. For both the customers and the trucks. We are greeted by the smell. Burning flesh. Wooden cages piled floor to ceiling. Dark and dank. Roosters screaming for a chance at the hens. Shivering fowl screaming for another chance. A decapitated bird, blood squirting from its neck, tries to escape. Momentarily, there is freedom until, exhausted from the loss of blood and lack of oxygen, it collapses at my feet. I am not afraid. After being killed, they are ready to be cleaned. Large cans that in a past life held olive oil have been engineered with little motorized fans and vacuum hoses. They suck the feathered birds in one end and release them out the other side, completely naked. It's fascinating. From there, they are dragged through a cold-water bath, dried, butchered, and wrapped. There are bunny rabbits cowering in a corner. "I didn't know we ate little bunnies," I say to my father. "Aunt Marion cooks them for New Year's," he says. "With olives. Tastes like chicken." I try not to be afraid.

I can smell the flowers in the funeral parlor now. Red hearts and white crosses. In my family, flowers meant death. My mother hated the smell. I hear my aunts, my mother. They are holding each other. Leaning on my uncles, my brother. They are pleading, shrieking. "No, papa, no. Please don't leave us." I think of the chickens. My eyes fill with tears. Begging, I say to my uncle, "I need to go home now. Please."

My Friend Billie

"You rat bastard!" he yelled, screaming so everyone could hear. The familiar sounds of Brooklyn coming from the next hooch. Right away, I felt less lonely. Less in danger. The girl-child we called Madame Nhu was putting away Billie's laundry, and she had shut the footlocker on his fingers. It was his way of dealing with the anger and the pain. There wasn't much to hold on to in Vietnam. No firm foundation. In a war, everything moves so fast, always spinning out of control. So hearing Billie scream, crossing paths with him again, was as reassuring to me as the two Etta James tapes I had carried 13,000 miles from home. Her stories like mine, touched by the white powder and brought to life through the magic of reel to reel.

We had first met when we were stationed at Fort Gordon, each dating one of the daughters of a local farmer. I walked onto the porch of their house on a Friday afternoon, and he was sitting with the girl's mother, shucking peas. He was going out with the younger one, Madge—everyone called her Maggie—and it looked like he was charming the pants off the older woman, as he had already done, he told me later, with her daughter. I wasn't having any such luck with her older sister, Jeanne, who liked to make out but didn't want to be touched down there. We had both been invited for dinner, a meal consisting of a roast chicken stuffed with dried fruits—which looked weird but tasted good—the peas, and a homemade loaf of braided bread. There were candles, and it seemed kind of festive; but then Max, their dad, closed his eyes and started praying. The prayers were in a language foreign to me, but Billie seemed to know a little. It helped that he had gone to Tilden, where nearly all his friends were Jewish. Having attended a great many Bar Mitzvahs, he already knew the blessings.

Before meeting Billie, I pretty much hung out with the black dudes, my racism having been tempered during my high school years at Hamilton and my time copping drugs. If you wanted to get high in the fifties, you had to deal with people of color. In my corner of Brooklyn, the blacks and the Puerto Ricans were the dealers on the street. When I was sent to rural Georgia, it was a major awakening that white people walked on one side of the avenue and everyone else, the other. Still, I was pissed when the fellas told me I couldn't go with them to a James Brown concert. That the concert venues were segregated. Inside the barracks, it was pretty much the same. There were two main groups in the army. The crackers from the South and the young bucks from the ghetto. The rest of us, hoods from the street and hicks from the prairie, were caught in the middle. The barracks were divided with bunks lined up on either side of a center aisle, and no one walked on the waxed floor. Where it was rare to talk across the divide, so guys like me had to pick a side. Given my life experience, my love for doo-wop, I chose to hang with the boys from the city.

I wasn't a grunt, but even my Vietnam wasn't a walk in the park. Vietnam was a very dicey place, and the war turned out to be as much about drugs as it was about death. Off base, you could get high every night. Smoke grass or shoot smack at the Crazy Horse Bar. At Tan Son Nhut, death arrived on the choppers throughout the day. Death hidden away in olive green plastic bags. Being with Billie at the dispensary when the body bags came in from the field was creepy. I had seen dead bodies at funerals, but body parts, that was a whole other level of scary. It really shook me up.

Billie was the base pharmacist and had his own jeep. We used it for trips to Saigon to sell tetracycline that he had stolen from the pharmacy. We knew a doctor named Shorty who passed it along to the rich and beautiful people with the clap. Gonorrhea was a growth industry, and we traded with the MPs for protection and with the mess sergeant for access to the kitchen. There we cooked and made believe we were still Italians in Brooklyn. We blew the profits partying in the clubs and on the B-girls at the Hollywood Bar. Dressed to look like American actresses and pinups, they entertained us and helped

us forget where we were. Fortunately, they never left me with the
need for our best-selling product.

Ford Fairlane

I hadn't thought of the car in years. Then one Saturday, in acting class, Rudi suggested we each describe our first car. For the next few minutes, as I waited my turn to speak, I found myself thinking about the car and my old girlfriend, Marie. My first real sexual relationship.

I didn't learn to drive until I was twenty-one. I had tried at sixteen on Billy's '53 Plymouth, but it was a disaster. It was the time he took me, Tony, and John to stay at his parents, cabin. The ice not yet thick enough to hold three of us tossing a football on the frozen Sound. We spent the weekend eating Chef Boyardee ravioli and drinking Four Roses. Canned pasta? I got so sick I thought I would die. None of us were very good at driving, but I was the one who burned out the clutch. So I learned some years later, driving a deuce and a half between the motor pool and the local beer stand on the strip outside the air base, on the road to Saigon.

A white 1959 Ford Fairlane was my first car. Red leather interior, taillights shaped like a sea creature, whitewalls, and '57 Plymouth hubcaps. Cost me $200, and I was looking good. This was late 1964, the year I met Marie. I had just returned from Vietnam, and the army, thank you, had stationed me twenty minutes from my mom's new house in Queens. She had been the last white holdout on the block and had sold our two-family in Brooklyn while I was in the war. I lived in the unfinished basement, a cellar really, and drove the Ford back and forth every day on the Interboro, now the Jackie Robinson Parkway. So even though I was in the army, wore fatigues, and took shit about getting my hair cut, I didn't eat army food or sleep on base. It was a great gig, and because I had talked my way into it—told the duty private I was married when I reported—it made me feel like I was on to something. I could talk the talk.

Marie and I were assigned to the same photography unit and had connected at an office Christmas party. I was a Spec-4, counting the days, and she was the captain's secretary. We had offered to close up shop so the others could get an early start on the holiday. An hour later, the lights were off, and we were half-naked and sweating as we ground our bodies into each other and the leather couch in the break room. I had a girlfriend, Carole, but she had been brain-washed at Catholic school and was saving it for marriage. Marie was already married, unhappily, she told me, and pleased that she had caught my attention.

Neither of us could afford a motel room, and we needed a place to go when we got together. That's where the Fairlane came in. Everyone I knew did it in cars. The leather was sticky, but I lifted a pink chenille spread from my mom to throw on the backseat. Marie made curtains for the windows, and I made a divider to separate front and back, to create the illusion of privacy. She had a picnic basket that we filled with wine and glasses, a couple of her son's cloth diapers, powder, lotion, and water. Sometimes she made cookies for a sweet treat after we had sex. On the nights she could get out, we met in Alley Pond Park, listened to the Beatles on a portable radio, and fucked the night away. I was young and horny. She was five years older, experienced and beautiful.

My mother was not happy I had two girlfriends. Worse, that one was married and had a kid. She wanted me to marry Carole, wanted a daughter. So when Marie broke up with me a year or so later, my mom was the first to congratulate me. By then the car had been vandalized, the radio stolen the night I copped grass in the old neighborhood. On a rainy June morning in 1970, I traded the car to Carole's brother Alan for his 1961 VW Bug. New hippie homeowners, we drove off to the country. We had dreams, we tried, open marriage and all, but we didn't have a clue. We broke up in 1974. Unfortunately, the marriage lasted only about as long as I owned the Ford.

The Clubhouse

We were slashing the little white ball back and forth across the green-painted plywood table. I've always loved ping-pong. The constant motion, offense-defense. You against the other. If you fuck up, you own it. Your responsibility. I can be a team player, but I'm not a doubles kind of guy. Partnerships are for relationships. I prefer to live by my own rules, make my own decisions. I'm not good at people telling me what to do. Probably why I didn't do so well in high school, or the army for that matter.

We were hanging out in the clubhouse. On the corner of Schaefer, in the buff-colored brick building owned by Mr. Perkins. It was the former home of the Amvets, an American veterans' organization that provided a place for returning soldiers to have a beer. Before they took their families and fled to the suburbs. Perks was a friend of Billy's father; he vouched for us, and we made a deal to take it over. Pay the rent of $25 a month. Three large rooms. A kitchen, a living room, and a game room. The coal stove that kept the place warm and the ping-pong table were in the same room. We were on the up-and-up, had a charter signed by Carmine DeSapio, the longtime New York Tammany Hall boss, that said we were the Democratic Social Club. We chipped in to buy it from some of those same Catholic guys running toward the Island. Away from the area and the black folks buying their houses to the green grasses of Levittown. We all chipped in, cost us $40 bucks.

We spent our time watching TV or making out if we had a girl. We were weekend warriors, and mostly what we did was shoot up, as the weekend stretched out to include Thursday and Wednesday and then Monday and Tuesday. Would just settle into one of those mid-century overstuffed chairs and nod the night away. Copped junk from Little Eddie, who hung out in the chicken joint down on Central. Eddie was my girlfriend Vanessa's cousin. I still think about her sometimes. How we walked up and down the block holding hands. Knowing that people were looking at us, checking us out between the venetian blinds. "What's a nice Italian boy like that doing with a colored girl?" First they said something to my mom, but she didn't worry about it too much; she was mostly thinking about how to put food on the table to feed me and my brothers. Then the priest from our parish approached my Uncle Nick and said it wasn't such a good idea. White and black went against the natural order, wasn't what God intended. Uncle Nick agreed. "Black and white is for spectator pumps," he said, invoking one of his tried-and-true fashion maxims. We had met when my mom rented out the upstairs apartment to Willie and Charlene. Vanessa watched their new baby after school so Charlene could work the night shift in the sweatshop where Uncle Nick was the presser. It was the house my parents bought in 1948. My father took the new Mercury when he left, but the judge wouldn't let him sell the house, so we had a place to live.

It was late. Vanessa had gone home, and there were just a couple of us around when me and Tony decided to score a little something. We shared a chicken sandwich, finished our business with Eddie, and were walking back to the club when a few black teenyboppers called us over. Wanted to bum a smoke. As I cupped a match to give one of the kids a light, this young boy, barely a teen—we were probably eighteen or nineteen—put a knife to my neck. Asked for money, and, besides, he wanted to know, "What the fuck you white boys doin on my block?" Now ain't that a kick in the ass, I thought. What goes around comes around. What am I gonna do now? So I started to talk. "Hey, what gang are you guys with? We ran with the Halsey Bops. Hung out in the park." Then I got lucky, said some magic words. "You know Little Eddie by any chance?" Eddie turned out to be the kid's uncle. Left him with my pack of Luckies, and we were on our way.

Me and Tony shared a nickel bag, then played ping-pong until it started to get cold. The fire dying down and the potbelly stove no longer cherry red. The coal bin on empty. We wrapped ourselves in fake Orientals, but we were freezing. Looking at each other, we knew in an instant what we had to do. I found a hatchet in the basement, and the table's legs were the first to go. The plywood top was harder to deal with, but we figured it out. We moved a couple of chairs up close, and I immediately felt the warmth on my black-sneakered feet. Throwing off the carpets, we nodded through slitted eyes while the stove's belly turned white and started to rumble. We joked about burning down the building, but the smack put us to sleep before the last flame flickered. I'm sure Perks was pissed when he came around to collect the next month's rent. Probably not as much as me, though, when I noticed that the soles on my new Pro-Keds had melted from the heat.

Unfinished Basement

First they knocked, then they pushed the door open. They probably said, "Police. Open up!" I'm not really sure. They entered with flashlights drawn, shining the lights in our eyes. "You," one of them said, looking at me. "You live here? Where are your parents?" No guns, shouting a little. Acting pretty casual, like this should be the worst of their problems. We were in the basement, playing loud music. Maybe the Drifters. A little beer. There were about ten of us. We had been dancing, making out. Someone shut the music. "I'll call my mom," I said.

She was upstairs in our first-floor apartment. I went to the stairs and yelled, "Ma, there's someone here to see you." She came down the basement stairs, kind of happy-go-lucky, she would have called it, but then got confused when she saw the cops. "Is everything alright? Is something wrong, officer?" she said. The older one, the dark one, stepped forward. "I'm sorry to have to tell you this, Mrs., uh, ma'am." "Gioia," she said, using her married name, still refusing to accept that her marriage to my father was over. "We've had complaints from some of your neighbors," he said. "These Christmas decorations," and he looked around at the colored lights shining through the windows, the decorated tree in the corner that covered up the mousetrap set with Parmesan. "These decorations may have been stolen." Busted! We looked at each other, me and Tony. Karen and Nina and John. This party was definitely over. My mother grabbed the older one's arm, started speaking Italian. I began to daydream, think of other parties. There was the one when I was five. Dressed in my little gray suit and matching brimmed hat. In that woman's house, I think her name was Rosalie, who had recently come from Italy. She lived across the street from us on Putnam Avenue. She was celebrating

All Saints' Day. Could little Frankie come over and spend the day imitating a saint? I played Joseph, who was the father of the baby Jesus. Who didn't get to sleep with the mother, played by Mary. She being extremely famous, even today, for the divine intervention that allowed her to have a baby without ever having gone all the way. It was a vegetarian feast, as I recall, mostly food that had been dipped in eggs, breaded, and fried in olive oil. The broccoli and cauliflower my particular favorites. We had to say some prayers, but mostly me and the other little saints played in the street. Whenever we came in to eat, the women would ooh and aah and take turns pinching our cheeks. And this past summer, when we celebrated my graduation from Catholic school. JoJo and Ann Marie had brought some beer and some 45s, but I couldn't dance because my cousin Lillian hadn't yet taught me the fox-trot. Then I heard the other cop ask my mom, "So where did these decorations came from?" "They're ours," she said. "I let the kids use them so they could celebrate the holiday. They're good kids, officer. I wouldn't lie to you." They looked at each other, and the Italian one said, "Thank you for your cooperation, Mrs. Gioia. Merry Christmas." Then they went out the same door they came in.

"Where did you get these?" my mom said in her angriest but still disbelieving voice. "We chipped in, Ma, all of us. We just wanted to have a party." "It's true, Mrs. Gioia," Tony lied. "We did." And she believed us because, more than anything, she wanted to. In fact, we had walked over a block or two. Most everyone had lights hanging from the windows, the doors. We were quiet, very careful. We took only the things we could easily carry. Strings of lights usually, disconnecting them from the end of their holiday display. Once, someone inside saw our reflection and shouted at us. It was frightening, but we cursed and laughed and ran like hell.

My mom yelled as she climbed the stairs, "You kids better be careful. Don't let me catch you getting into trouble again. You hear me, Frankie?" She went up to the kitchen, returned with another tray of lasagna. Someone turned the music back on, and we started dancing. "Eat," she said. "It's a party, right?" We ate, we danced, made out and did the grind until around midnight. Unfortunately, when I woke up in the morning, I was still a virgin. What are you gonna do? Catholic girls.

Just a Little R & R

They walked into the office real casual-like. The lieutenant colonel, followed by the captain. Maybe he was a full bird, I honestly don't remember. Usually, when a senior officer is around, you get a heads-up. Not this time. The captain, all smiles as he made the introductions. "Sir, this is Specialist Gioia. The soldier you were asking about." Really, he was asking about me? That can't be good. The colonel held out his hand. "It's a pleasure to meet you, young man. I want you to know your work hasn't gone unnoticed at HQ." So they knew who I was, another soldier in the fight. Vietnam. Not something that thrilled me . . . the less people knew your name, the better.

When I joined the army, they assigned me to the Signal Corps for advanced training. But I failed out of a technical repair course and was being transferred when someone noticed that my administrative scores were off the charts. So after threatening me with three years in the Infantry, they decided to try me in Supply. Like Klinger. While I couldn't figure out if a transistor was bad, and which one, if any, had to be replaced, I knew how to make sure it was in stock and how to locate it when it was needed.

The colonel went on to say that because of the system I had developed, very few choppers were being grounded. In fact, it was so effective, he was sending me to Soc Trang, in the Mekong Delta, to teach it to the supply team down there. I would probably get a medal. A regular superhero. "Look at it as a little R & R," he said. I should be at the airfield early to catch the first flight out. Then he said, "Be careful, young fella, and good luck." Be careful? Good luck? That didn't sound very reassuring. Until then, I had refused all offers to go for rides on the helicopters. Hueys were always being shot down, so the smart move was to stay on the ground.

A camouflaged C-47 transport plane, with "Puff the Magic Dragon" painted on the fuselage, was loading when I got there. I found a seat and settled in among the skids of cargo and bloated green mailbags. I was feeling pretty anxious, freaking out to be honest, but we took off from Saigon without a hitch. During the two-hour flight we all relaxed a little, talked about going home, and chain-smoked like it was our last puff. Because, hey, you never know. Then I noticed the sacks of letters, letters that could have crossed in the mail. "Dear Johnny," it might say. "How are you? We miss you very much." The reply delivered by men in dress khaki, standing at attention. "Dear Mr. and Mrs. . . . a grateful nation mourns your loss." As the plane began its descent, we could hear the sounds of pop, pop all around us. I was scared shit, but it's not like there was anything I could do. Then one of the journalists who was hitching a ride told me to get ready. When the plane's wheels touched down, the rear cargo door opened, and the plane accelerated. The skids rolled out the opening, and we ran toward the light, against the forward movement of the plane. When my feet hit the ground, I immediately fell on my ass. Dazed, I saw the plane gain altitude, heard the popping sounds again, and watched the fireworks explode against the blue sky. This is not what I had in mind. I mean, where in hell have they sent me?

I spent three days in the Delta, constantly on edge. I barely slept —if you don't count the time I took a nap—while sitting in a chair, drinking a rum and Coke in the shower. Like some rock and roll gig at the Paramount, the light show began every evening, as day turned to night. Tracer rounds lit up the dark sky, and mortars whizzed by overhead. "Don't let it get you down, man," one of the guys I met there told me. "The VC are just letting us know they're out there. We may control this little strip of land, but this is their country, and they will kick our asses out before we know it." "That works for me," I said. "What are we doing here anyway? They can have this godforsaken jungle. Yeah, book me a ticket to ride. As long as I'm traveling upright, get me the fuck out of here."

Barney's Express

I never met Sammy the Bull, but I did know Johnny Boy, Dominick the Skinny, and Angie. We had dropped out of high school, and worked together in the garment center, for Barney's Express. I told my mom I was quitting the day some black guys started shooting at one another. With people carrying guns, it became way too hairy to even walk to the train after eighth period. My father, who spent his working life driving a truck, got me a job as a trucker's helper. Johnny Boy worked as my dad's helper. I worked with Angie.

It was around the time I quit the Halsey Bops. Deciding that night at Lefty's house, after I asked to borrow his gun. The Beretta he always carried when he made collections. His wife, Mary, didn't pull any punches. "Lefty, are you crazy?" she yelled. Then she stared at me and said, "What if something happens to you? What about your mother?" She was shaking her head, cursing under her breath, and letting us know she was totally disgusted. "Why are you doing this," she said, "wasting your time gang fighting? You're sixteen, for Chrissake. You should be going out with girls." Lefty was laid back as usual, casually mentioning that if I hurt somebody, I could go to jail. Getting my attention but letting me figure it out myself, which fortunately I did.

Angie was pissed at me, couldn't get over the fact that I had been with the Halsey Bops. Didn't like that we tried to coexist with the Bishops from Bed-Stuy and some of the other black gangs. He, Johnny, and Dom were with Fulton and Rockaway, an Italian crew that fought those boys day after day, block by block, as they moved into what had been white areas of Brooklyn. So although Johnny couldn't have cared less, even told him to cool it, Angie let me know that he thought I was a punk and a nigger lover for not wanting to fight the Bishops anymore. He called me a fat fuck and a pussy and taunted me by knocking cigarettes out of my mouth. I hated that I let him get away with it, and I wished I'd had the balls to smash his face in, but he scared me.

This was a complete turnaround for me. When I was growing up, I had been one of the tough guys. If you didn't live on Schaefer Street and tried to cross my block, I was always ready to fuck with you. Like those fucking Murphy brothers, candy-asses that they were. Irish boys. Each one taller than the next, with arms that almost touched the ground. I had known them years earlier when we spent long summer days playing stickball. When it was still all about the Dodgers and the Giants. They were Yankee fans. This was before the gangs and before the white lady began to steal our lives. For a time, when I was about ten, stickball was my life. I would wait until it got light, but by eight in the morning I was ringing Ferrara's bell. His grandmother would crack open the apartment door, the smells from the previous day's cooking hitting me in the face, enough to make me nauseous. The old woman, still in her housecoat, would stick out her leathered, frog-like face and wonder what I wanted. No, her grandson wasn't up yet. Yes, she would tell him I had come by. We needed him if we hoped to have any chance of beating those boys from over on Moffat Street. Now these clowns thought they could just waltz down my block whenever they wanted. Bullshit. Not without us at least getting in their faces, making them think about it, so they shivered a little before they tried it the next time. But I was not into fighting Angie. He was a gorilla, bigger and stronger than me, and unpredictable. He would just lose it for no reason, so I knew it wasn't a good idea to fuck with him. Not for nothing they called him Quack Quack.

Some years later there was a hit on the Gambino family crime boss, Big Paulie. It was major, front page in the *Daily News*. The papers said that it had been arranged by Johnny Boy. Guys in suits visited local shopkeepers. "Close down tomorrow," they suggested. "Show some respect." There were big changes coming in the family. Before long, the papers started referring to Johnny Boy as the Dapper Don.

Then I thought back to that day on Thirty-Eighth Street, when Barney's son, Aaron, let Johnny take his car for a drive. A pink, 1959 Chrysler convertible. The price tag still in the window, the car smelling of leather. Johnny behind the wheel, so sure of himself and knowing that he should get used to this. That one day he would be treated like royalty. Then he announced, "If I had this car, I'd have to sweep the chicks out with a broom." And me and everyone else standing there, young and old alike, laughed and nodded, because we all knew, he was already a star.

Angie? He died in '89. Cancer. Saw it in the *Post*. I remember, because I tried very hard not to smile.

Next Stop . . . Red Hook

I'd been surfing the net, looking for information on my long-ago gang, the Halsey Bops. Checking the history, the night Gotti and his boys from Fulton and Rockaway had saved our asses from the Corsair Lords. The bazaar at the church. Instead, a picture of the Savages wearing their colors. People dancing in what looked like a finished basement. It's an Italian thing. Buy a brick house and, first thing, finish the basement. Keep the kids at home. We could dance, drink, and make out a little. An adult or two would be upstairs, so there was definitely no fucking. We were Catholic, after all. It was probably one of the reasons we all got married so young.

I checked out the picture but didn't recognize anyone. Then, right there in the corner, sitting on a ratty old couch, was a guy who looked like me. An Elvis impersonator. In the '50s, Elvis was my calling card. But why was I in this picture? Then I remembered Donna. We had met at the old Madison on Myrtle. A Sunday matinee of *Some Like It Hot*. I usually went to the movies with Tony or John. They were the best at picking up girls. I was self-conscious about being overweight, so I tried to play it cool, often ended up with the shy one. Donna wasn't shy though; she was totally into it. She was visiting her cousin, didn't live in the area. Said she lived in Red Hook. I mean, where the fuck is Red Hook?

When the movie was over, we went to Shanghai Palace next door, where Kenny had taken us to a drag show once to celebrate his birthday. We felt worldly. A certain step up from Tony's coffee shop. Later, Donna gave me her number and invited me to her sweet sixteen the following Saturday. She had given me reason to think she could be the one. Sitting in the balcony, I had my hand under her sweater in no time. She even helped me unhook her bra. This wouldn't be easy though. I would have to take the BMT local and go two stops to Myrtle. Then catch the A train into Manhattan. I would need to change at Fourteenth Street, go south to Park Slope, and down to the waterfront. The place was an industrial nightmare. It would take me an hour and a half to get there, and it would be forever getting back home. On the bright side, if I scored, it would be worth it. I wore my new three-button jacket and a rayon shirt the color of cappuccino. A pinch bottle of Smirnoff's in the inside pocket. I rang the bell and waited. Her mother answered the door. "Hi," I said. "I'm Frankie, a friend of Donna's." Poker-faced, she just stood there, checking me out. Then she reached over and hugged me. Her breasts pressed against my chest, then slid up and settled under my chin. Just like my Tittie Rosie's. When she released me, she smiled, placed her hands on my face, squeezed my cheek, and said, "My Donna said you were such a nice a boy. Italiano?" Then she yelled, "Donna, your friend is here" and told me all the kids were downstairs. I didn't know anyone, and when I realized the place was filled with people from South Brooklyn gangs, it freaked me out. Even though mostly everyone was Italian, I knew how that could go. I mean, this wasn't my turf, and the Halsey Bops weren't exactly welcome in Red Hook.

I found an upstairs bathroom, sat on the toilet, and cracked the seal on my vodka. It gave me a little courage and a little buzz. Then I went to look for Donna. I found her in the bedroom in front of a lighted mirror, putting on makeup. She smiled when she saw me but didn't say a word. So I stood by the door and watched. She licked her lips and put on blood-red lipstick. I watched her breasts make an appearance when she bent over to put on her socks. Checked out her body as she turned to appraise her skin-tight dungarees in the mirror. Then I heard footsteps, and when I turned, I heard her mother yell, "Donna, what are you doing?" She wasn't smiling. How long had she been standing there? Donna started to close the door. I stepped back, wished her a happy birthday, turned and took the stairs down two at a time. I waited an hour for the fucking train.

Playland or Land of Play

There must have been close to twenty of us on the train. Mostly Halsey Bops, the guys and girls who hung out in the park. The A train to the Rockaways, the beach at Ninety-Sixth Street. Where we went swimming during the day and walked under the massive, grinning clown of the now long-gone Playland at night. The guys wearing paisley-print button-downs and the girls in pedal pushers and one-piece swimsuits. Where me and the gang walked the boardwalk, looking to throw a punch, or ran around on the sand throwing a football.

Little Frankie was on that train, and and so were Vicky and Gina. The first trip of summer to the ocean. Frankie was good people, and we were close. We played basketball for 14 Holy Martyrs, and after games we would go to his house, smoke pot, and listen to Elvis and the Platters. I was surprised to see Vicky and Gina though. They were older, and usually drove around in Gina's white Caddy with the top down. They were together, as usual, their hair teased to the heavens, eyes outlined in mascara and purple shadow. Wearing skimpy tops and white short-shorts that had been rolled up to the V of their thighs. Not a tan line in sight, testifying to the fact that they spent their days on the rooftops across from the playground worshipping the sun gods. We had barely settled into our seats, carrying our coolers and blankets, when Gina got up, smiled at Frankie, whispered in his ear, and the two of them walked to the other end of the subway car. I guess she had a plan, because they slid into one of those private seating areas at the end of the car, and they stayed in that cubbyhole for over an hour, making out and who knows what else. Didn't show themselves again until we got to Rockaway. Little Frankie had a smile a mile wide. Gina didn't look too shabby either.

On the beach, we smoked some grass, drank a few beers, and soaked up the sun. At twilight we walked over to Playland to check out the rides. I wasn't feeling any pain, and I got on the line for the Ferris wheel. I was afraid of heights, so normally I would have just gone on the bumper cars. Lots of fun, but not what you would call risky. As the line got shorter, I started to have second thoughts. When I looked up, me and Vicky were next, so I went for it. I couldn't let her see that I was afraid. When we reached the top, probably a hundred feet from the ground, I held on tight to the lap bar and tried not to scream. Just sat still, closed my eyes, and waited for it to end. When I felt Vicky's hand over mine, I started to relax. I always appreciated that she never brought it up, or told anyone.

On the subway ride home, it didn't take long for Gina to get everyone's attention. She was holding on to one of the train's center poles . . . rubbing herself against it. I guess she had taken a few substances herself, because then she points and says, "Hear me out, people. I'll buy a three- piece suit for the first guy who goes down on me." Looking around with her sexy smile, while Vicky laughed. "That's right, you heard me. A three-piece suit." In the late fifties, a three-piece suit, which included a vest, was one of the hippest styles in men's fashion. Jackie, one of the older guys, spoke up right away. "Hey, Gina, just say the word, and I'll eat you out whenever you're ready, babe. And you can ask around, I don't come up until I look like a frosted donut."

On the train, people couldn't stop talking about whether they were serious. I mean, everyone knew Gina was outrageous, but Jackie was a drug addict. He shot a couple of bags of dope every day. So you couldn't be sure with him. Still, he had a steady job, working the dining room at Red's Bakery and Pizzeria. During the week as a waiter and as the maitre d' on weekends. A couple of weeks later, me and Little Frankie showed up at Red's on a Saturday night. Jackie greeted us at the door with a big smile. Done up in a silk tie, with a pocket square placed just so, wearing a brand-new, gray-pin-striped three-piece suit.

Seventeen

I was up half the night telling myself that I wasn't sure I could write this story. Tell this story. It happened almost sixty-five years ago. You're probably wondering, How can he be so sure? I'm sure because I was there, and I'll never forget what happened. I spent a lot of time that day standing in the street, waiting around with the other guys. I can still hear them saying, "I'm next," and I can still feel the knot in my stomach. Makes me feel queasy again, like I felt on that hot summer day. The day that turned to night. And because I was just a scared kid, probably twelve or thirteen, and it didn't seem right, I didn't get in line.

The scene of the crime was a 1940s Plymouth. It was parked in the rusted tin garage near the corner with Central, down the block from my house. Across the alley from Zito's grocery. The place where I had my first job, if you don't count my gig peeling potatoes at the fish market. I worked until six and made like two bucks, that I used to buy a pizza at Red's place. Brought it home for dinner, for the family. Made me feel like a big shot. Zito's was the place where we went for hero sandwiches. Salami and provolone with yellow mustard on half a loaf of Italian bread. They cost twenty-five cents, and Patsy the butcher let us hang out in the back. Gave us a beer to share, to help wash it down.

It started with Sal, who could dance like Gene Kelly and was my friend Nick's older brother. The Plymouth was Sally's car. The car had a rumble seat that he let us sit in when he took us for rides around the neighborhood. We laughed, waved to people we knew, yelled at those we didn't. Yeah, it started with Sal taking Anna for a drive. Just the two of them, maybe to Highland Park, both of them smiling. When they came back a little while later, he pulled the car into the garage. I heard the garage door open, heard it scraping on the ground. Then I heard Anna. She was about fifteen and had come with her family from Germany. She spoke halting English, but she was a looker, as they used to say about girls who seemed to have it all back then. She had a great figure, regular Coke-bottle stuff. Tall with long legs and blonde hair down her back. We called her Anna Banana because, like her, the name had sexual content. She wore tight dungarees and sweaters that showed it off. Which was the style in the '50s and what all the girls who went to Catholic school wore. They were sitting in the car, and through the screen door out back I heard Sal say, "C'mon Anna, all the girls do it. You know how much I like you, and you wanna be like American girls, right?" I imagined that Anna sighed, maybe smiled weakly through closed lips, and even though she wasn't convinced, said, "Yes, like American girls."

After about twenty minutes or so, Sal came out of the garage, laughing and jumping around. Saying to a few of the guys, "Of course we did it. She loved it. She's a real tiger, that one. Couldn't get enough of me." Then he got this satisfied look and said, "I rest my case." He tapped one of his buddies on the shoulder, "Go ahead, man. She's waiting for you. Where's my brother?" He yelled, "Hey, Nicky, you're next." The word got out real fast, and before long there was a line of guys standing in the street. Laughing and horsing around while they waited their turn. The number seventeen sticks in my head. I never saw Anna again. They said the family moved to New Jersey. I wonder sometimes, does she still think about what happened to her? What they did to her.

Then I thought back to my first time. With Kathleen, in the schoolyard. Not the one at the parochial school. I would never do it by the Catholic church, not with God watching. We did it around the corner, by the basketball courts at PS 85. Freezing cold. Me saying, "C'mon Kath. You know how I feel about you. You know you wanna do it too." But did she really? I know she didn't say no.

Fort Totten

The volume on the radio was turned to the max. Me and Mary Wells singing "My Guy." I got off the Clearview and wheeled onto Bell Boulevard. I could see the rolling hills up ahead, hugging Little Neck Bay. It looked like a college campus, not an army base. What a score! Fort Totten. A place where even while playing golf, a general could order missiles to be fired from Greenland to attack the then Soviet Union. The perfect pastoral setting, where old commanders could go to die, or have their pictures taken. Whichever came first. My bonus for having given a year to the cause. Vietnam. A year that kept me constantly on edge but also provided drugs to get me high or calm me down. It's where I met Jackie, and with her guidance, my sexual fantasies became sexual experiences. Where I learned to embrace the concept practice makes perfect.

The guard on duty waved me through, and I followed the signs to headquarters. I had this idea to live off base. To live in my mom's basement at the new house in Queens. Brooklyn having become enemy territory. On my left hand was the recently purchased wedding band that cost me a buck at a flea market. Army regulations. You had to be married to live off base. I was wearing my dress khakis, the Vietnam patch on my right arm, telling those in the know that I had served in a combat zone. The fruit salad on my chest, proof that I had endured and returned to collect my just reward. It was just past seven, so only the charge of quarters, probably a private, would be in the office.

This was going to be easy, I thought, as I handed the CQ my orders. He acted totally bored until he looked up and saw me. "Vietnam, huh? That must have been badass." All upbeat now and wanting to make conversation. "How was it over there?" "How was it?" I said sarcastically. "You been reading the papers, man? People are dying in that hellhole. They just sent a quarter of a million more guys over there." "Fuck," he replied. "I thought it was all about guys getting high and getting laid. Like *M*A*S*H* or something. I mean, I didn't know it was that bad." "Bad doesn't begin to cover it," I said. "Seeing those body bags every morning can fuck with your head. The green bags, the morning light. Just parts . . . like jelly, man." We stood silent for a moment, looking past each other. I thought about the lieutenant who tried to get me to extend my tour. A first louie, new to the war. We were riding in the company jeep. He was driving like he had a new toy to play with. I was a short-timer, carrying my swagger stick and counting the days. Just thinking about going home. He looks over and says to me, "You know, soldier, I could really use your smarts over here. Re-up. Give me six months, and I'll make you a sergeant. Think about it." Yeah, right. Stateside babes, dinner at six. That's what I thought about. Then the private got up and extended his right hand. "I'm sorry if I . . . I didn't mean no disrespect." "Thanks," I said. "We're cool. It's just that I didn't know if I'd be sitting up for the flight home. You know what I'm sayin?"

I raised my left hand so he couldn't miss the wedding band on my ring finger. Turned it with the thumb and forefinger of my right. "Anyway, I married my sweetie when I got back, so I'll be living off base. What time is reveille?" He smiled. "Damn! Don't that beat all! Congratulations! I know some broads don't wait. You need a parking sticker for your car?" "Yeah, sure. It's a '59 Ford." I pointed out the window to my Fairlane. "The white one? I like those taillights," he said. "Looks like some kinda marine species, like you could drive underwater." "Yeah, like a shark," I mumbled. "You need anything else? I'm kind of beat." "No, we're good," he said. "Just so you know, first call is at eight. The first sergeant gets in after he plays nine." I turned to leave and heard him say, "Hey, can I ask ya somethin? Didja kill any gooks over there?" I didn't answer, just kept walking to my car.

Jerry's Funeral

He didn't look much different. Wearing a blue pin-striped suit, a conservative dark tie. Straight gray hair combed back on the sides. He had that same smile, the devilish smirk he got when he lowered his eyes and stared at an attractive woman. He could be telling a story about going to the track, maybe how he hit the daily double at Belmont. Could be walking into a family celebration, dressed to the nines, or just sitting on a couch watching baseball. He was always a presence. People noticed him. He had just turned eighty.

My kid brother called to tell me. "Dad died," he said. "A heart attack." His voice flat as always. "Are you coming down for the funeral? Me and Pat are gonna go. Joe said he and Kathy are gonna come in too. You and Susie can stay at our house if you want." So we went. Three brothers and their wives. Trying to understand that long-ago time. The anger that seduced my personality. My feelings of abandonment and the sadness of missed opportunity.

The funeral parlor was on Long Island, in an old colonial on the highway to Montauk. There were other people in the viewing room, people I didn't know. A few older women with their adult daughters sitting toward the front. "He was such a nice man," one of them said. "He made coffee at the senior center every morning." The woman next to her replied, "And he loved children. Always playing with my grandson. Do you know? Did Jerry have children?" "Yeah, he had them, lady," I answered. "There's three of us . . . and he couldn't have given a fuck less about us. What else do you want to know? That he was a self-centered son of a bitch?" And I sat back down, trembling.

He left us when I was going on twelve. Drove that new blue Mercury down the block and out of our lives. I joined the Halsey Bops that fall and at fifteen started hanging out in the poolroom.

I was skin-popping before my sweet sixteen. Five years of watching my guys OD before joining the army at twenty. By then it was time to break out of the weekend-warrior culture. My mom tried Valium, but she never recovered from the sorrow and the pain. The shame. It was impossible to go back to the way it was before—before my dad started sleeping with my Aunt Betty, his kid brother's wife. We hadn't seen him in years. Our kids were already in high school. He arrived unannounced, driving a trailer and towing a girlfriend, to visit us in Great Barrington. It reminded me of one of those sometime visits he made to see us when we were kids. Maybe once a month, although we waited every weekend. "I'll be there by eleven," he would say on the old rotary. Don't bet on it. Even though I wanted to see him, I hated it when he showed up. He would have my Aunt Betty and her kids with him. I wanted to beat the shit out of my cousins. Like it was their fault that my father was a whore and their mother was a tramp. He wanted to see Damien, he said. Wanted to spend some time with his grandson. Came for a day and sheepishly asked if they could stay for the weekend. When he left, he said he'd see us again soon. Yeah, right. It was the last time I saw him. Before that day. Lying in that box.

I was daydreaming, all curled up in the mohair, as my brother Jerry maneuvered the Caddy onto the Southern State. Thinking about the time my father had invited me to his new house to have dinner with him. The new family. Aunt Betty and her four kids. He stood over a pot of fish soup and held court. Told stories about taking me to the local gin mill when I was still wearing short pants. Me sitting up on the bar, drinking a Coke. He had that same magnetic quality. Then I heard my brother from the driver's seat say, "Ya know about Aunt Betty's kids, right? The young ones, Jackie and Gary. The *J* and the *G*, the same initials as Dad's, *Jerry Gioia*. She named them after him. Ya know what I'm sayin?" I didn't answer. I thought they were my cousins, but fuck . . . maybe they're my brothers!

He Was the First

Merchandising was not something I knew anything about. Not until I met up with JoJo and Ann Marie again. I hadn't seen them since the summer I joined the Halsey Bops. I stared, actually leered, at them and could smell their sex in the humid heat. They smiled, killer smiles, but in an instant it was all business. JoJo purred, "The red ones are fifty cents; the orange ones, three for two dollars. Down two with half a bottle of cough medicine, and mimic the white magic." It sounded good, was cheaper than a $5 bag, and you didn't have to take a bus to Williamsburg to score. Plus you could say "Fuck you" to the cops, who were looking to bust your sweet ass, and the chacho, who wanted a taste. Walking away, I wondered if maybe, just maybe, we could get high together and lay our heads on each other's shoulders.

Donnie drove, Tony's older brother. We let him hang out with us because he had a license and a red and black '53 Buick. Tony and I were partners. Your partner was someone you shared your drugs with, your money, and your secrets with, the person you trusted to take care of you if anything went wrong. The person who would call your mother if it came to that. We hugged and kissed like Sicilian cousins, and only Tony's father thought we were fags. We took the Grand Central to Alley Pond Park, downed two Seconals, and shared a bottle of Robitussin AC. Settling into the leather for another night among the suburban kids, making out to the sounds of Little Anthony. In minutes, the drugs sent me spiraling into a deep nod. Nodding is like dreaming, except there is no plot. Nothing substantive. I opened my eyes five hours later, unaware that I had lost another day from my life. I wiped the three-inch-long Lucky Strike ash from between my burned, orange fingers, peed, and scratched my pancake-colored skin until the blood slowly seeped back into my veins. A still-stoned Donnie let me drive the Buick to the diner on 110th Street and Atlantic Avenue. The sudden glare of the grimy overhead lights forced my eyes to focus, and the scene was bleak. *The Snake Pit* came to mind. John and Eugene were at a corner booth, looking like they were ready to be autopsied. Eugene, scratching his scrawny face until the pimples on his cheeks bled to match the vinyl. John, just minutes removed from shooting up, with a vacant stare on his ghostlike face. Mindlessly stirring a steady stream of sugar into his coffee, while the steaming liquid ran over the cup, across the red Formica table, over his balls, down his leg, and onto the checkerboard tiled floor.

Earlier that night, they had run into a nickel bag at the poolroom. Not content with just being stoned, they had cooked behind the diner and booted up under a lamppost. John, especially, was always looking to raise the bar. Stoned was never high enough; he always wanted to get totally wasted. When word of a cough medicine, downs, and junk cocktail got around, it became the choice of anyone looking to fly off into another world. Unfortunately, it left many of the guys without a return ticket home. That winter, John and Eugene began dealing a selection of ups and downs to support their worsening heroin habits. They also continued to mix and match drugs, like choosing dishes from columns A and B. On a frigid December night, they settled in to John's '57 Pontiac to shoot a bag of junk that looked like brown sugar. We found them the following morning, as their skin color turned from white to blue and black. A collection of pills, red ones and orange ones, glowed against the car's black shag carpeting. We rolled them in the snow, rubbed ice on their balls, and smacked them silly, but only Eugene shivered in the ten-degree cold.

John Ferrara was the first guy I knew to wear a sports jacket for no apparent reason. No wedding or funeral to go to, but just because he thought it was cool. We were twelve. He was the first guy on our block to get a blow job. He got cum on his blue school pants and wore them like a badge. He noticed that Rocky always giggled when he shot pool, and he found out why. The next weekend, five of us crouched under a blanket in Rock's apartment and got high on grass for the first time. From the beginning, as young kids playing stickball, everyone wanted to be his best friend, including me. In the winter of our nineteenth year, he died. He was the first.

I Was in a War Once

I met a guy at a party a few years ago, and he told me I probably had PTSD. "What are you talking about, man? No way," I laughed. "Whatever you're smoking, I want some." "Post-Traumatic Stress Disorder," he said. "I mean, pretty much everybody who was in Vietnam has it. The government, they pay me, like, over a grand a month. You just have to get checked out." "Fuck that," I said. "I'm fine. Besides, there's no way I let Uncle Sam back into my life for a few bucks." But on the drive home, I started to think about that time at the movies. It was after I moved to the Berkshires from the Catskills. After I met Susie on the train. More than a decade had passed, and we were worrying about our kids having to register for the draft. I was taking classes with the American Friends Service Committee so we could figure out a way for our boys to beat it. We went to see *Born on the Fourth of July* at the Mahaiwe—the old heating system chugging along, trying but failing to raise the temperature a degree or two.

I spent a year in Vietnam as a twenty-year-old. While I was still a boy. Coming home, no longer a boy. Getting out just as the Gulf of Tonkin episode turned into an excuse to fight a real war. I can still see the general in the mess hall, his chest covered with campaign ribbons and flashing lots of shiny brass. For me, it was still a country-club war then. Cooking Italian food in the company kitchen, getting high with Billie, and spending long Saturdays with Jackie in her room. But my most searing memory, the thing I'll never forget, was the body bags. Lying on the ground, tagged and waiting to be shipped home. The fear of flying horizontal.

I don't go to the movies much. The smell of make-believe butter on designer popcorn makes me nauseous. I was sitting there hugging myself, trying to get warm, when I felt my chest tighten. I couldn't breathe. I was still a young man, only forty-seven, but I thought I was having a heart attack. A few seconds later, I was running down the steep, narrow stairs to the men's room. Sitting on the toilet and crying my eyes out. Not knowing why. It happened again a few months later. I was driving across the Hudson, listening to NPR. It was 1990, the first Iraq war. Saddam had invaded Kuwait, and Poppy Bush had sent troops to the Middle East. There was a report about soldiers fighting the oil fires, how the intense heat was scarring their lungs . . . shortening their lives. First I teared up, and in no time I was bawling.

I started to write this piece on December 18, 2016, a day after seeing an obit in the *Berkshire Eagle*. The deceased guy had been in Vietnam. They said he tried to protect the Vietnamese from the horror at My Lai, when, on March 16, 1968, at least three-hundred men, women, and children had been massacred by U.S. forces. The tears started to run down my face. Now the military patrols our southern border. To protect us from the brown people trying to escape a different kind of war.

Last month I wrote a piece about coming home from Vietnam. How I conned some hick private into believing I was married so I could live off base. In the story, I was young Frankie again, a Brooklyn tough guy. I started to tell the story to Susie, and the tears just flowed. The men in my family only cried at funerals, so I'm not sure when I received that gift. I'm not a tough guy anymore. It's hard sometimes, but to be able to feel pain also allows me to feel joy. I never fired my weapon in Vietnam. Never was shot at. But I heard the mortars overhead, felt the fear of knowing places I had been were bombed, and carried my anxiety every second of every day. The war was an experience that never leaves me. Vietnam was more than fifty years ago, but the crying, the heartache, and the guilt never end. I never know when grief might decide to pay me a visit. I am not a blank page.

Uncle Carmine

I want to tell you about my old friend Mikey. It's March 1966, and more than a year has passed since I got back from the war. I'm watching the Mets, spring training baseball on TV. The doorbell rings, and my mom comes in with a worried look on her face. "There's someone at the door," she says. "He's all dressed up. In a suit." Normally, she would just yell from the hall. So I think, Shit, maybe it's the cops. I go to the door, and it's Mikey. Done up in gray sharkskin, a felt hat, white-on-white shirt, silk tie, and wing tips. Cops and gangsters, they tend to dress alike, but gangsters wear far better clothes.

As promised, Mikey has shown up at my mother's new house. He was a mess sergeant in the army, and in Vietnam we were close. He was very into the war part and referred to himself as a combat cook. He would take hot food on the Hueys and deliver it to our boys in the field. Mikey always carried a loaded forty-five and talked all the time about wanting to be attacked by the Viet Cong. Then he could use his weapon, maybe win a medal or, at the very least, kill a few slopes. We connected around the Italian part, but the gun stuff was weird, and, to tell the truth, I always thought he was a little strange.

We sit and talk about the war, the future, and then he asks me, "So what are you gonna do now?" He reminds me of how we talked in Vietnam about Uncle Carmine. Mikey is still a soldier on the outside, a soon to be made man. He works for the Gambino family in Brooklyn. He's in charge of all fireworks sales in the city. Drives a new Buick, has an apartment in Manhattan and a live-in girlfriend. A nice girl, Mikey says, not someone his mother would approve of, but she'll do until the right Catholic virgin comes along. Me, I don't have a job, live at home, and I've begun to dabble in drugs again.

Just a few pills and cough medicine, but I've been there, and have to get it right this time. I'm trying to reinvent myself as a businessman, but I didn't go to college, and my army medals don't mean shit in the real world.

So I listen to Mikey talk. He wants me to meet Uncle Carmine—also known as the Doctor, because he fixes things. Uncle Carmine is a capo in the family. A big earner, he runs the rackets in Brooklyn. Besides fireworks, he's involved in hijacking, stock fraud, and loan-sharking. His picture is in the papers almost every day. The feds are after him, but Mikey tells me, "They can't do shit to him; he's got the fucking cops and the judges in his pocket. He's like the mayor of Brooklyn, for Chrissake." He's told him about me, and he's sure if I want a job, I've got it. If I'm game, we can go to his office at Alberto's clam bar later that night. Where I come from, an intro, a sit-down with a captain in the family, was a big deal. This was a career opportunity, something I definitely had to consider. Like how those of us who went to Catholic school considered the priesthood.

I knew a little about the Mob because of my cousin Lefty. Lefty was a big shot with the Teamsters . . . always traveled with two bodyguards. *Paisans,* sharp dressers, with bulges in their leather jackets. I think back to the time I went to his place as a teenager. His wife Mary cooked; we ate, drank wine. Then I asked if I could borrow the gun he carried for a big gang fight. Mary screamed, but Lefty was relaxed and said, "Sure, if you think that's a good idea." Then he said, "Just remember, now that you're sixteen, if you hurt somebody, they could burn you. You could burn, Frankie, burn." He scared the shit out of me, and when I said goodnight, I left the gun on the table. I'm thinking about that now and how my mom would always say, "He's a good boy, my Frankie. He's gonna make me proud." I turn towards Mikey, but he's already looking in the mirror, adjusting his fedora. We hug. He kisses me on both cheeks and says, "Don't forget, only someone you can trust will tell you when your face is dirty." I never see Mikey again.

Acknowledgements

"Food for Thought," "Powder-Blue Pants," and "Giuseppe" have appeared in the online magazine *Ovunque Siamo*. An earlier version of "Christmas Eve" was published in *The Artful Mind*.

I am extremely grateful for my son Damien. Being his father has been a blessing.

To my mom for always caring about us, for the confidence she had in me, and for her perseverance in the face of very difficult odds.

Thanks to Meradith of The Troy Book Makers for helping to make this book a reality.

To my friend Judi Kales for her superb copy editing of my manuscript. Her interest in working to get this book to its finished state made it easy.

Many thanks to Deb Koffman for providing a venue where area artists are able to share their work at her open mic. IWOW has been a treasure.

I have many memories of my cousin Sonny. Lefty to his friends, he was my idol growing up. He was always there to teach me the things I needed to know.

I still remember listening to jazz for the first time in Rocky's apartment. Thanks, Rock, for exposing me to the creative side of life.

Thank you to my wife Susie for her unending love and support of my artistic dreams. I couldn't have done it without you.

About the Author

FRANK GIOIA is a writer, actor, and playwright. His writing has been published in *Ovunque Siamo* and *The Artful Mind*. He reads his work regularly at an open mic, IWOW (In Words Out Words), in Housatonic, Massachusetts. A staged reading of his play *14 Holy Martyrs* was performed in the Berkshires in 2016.

VIA Folios

A refereed book series dedicated to the culture of Italians and Italian Americans.

STEVEN BELLUSCIO. *Constructing a Bibliography*. Vol 37. Italian Americana.

ANTHONY JULIAN TAMBURRI, Ed. *Italian Cultural Studies 2002*.
Vol 36. Essays.

BEA TUSIANI. *con amore*. Vol 35. Memoir.

FLAVIA BRIZIO-SKOV, Ed. *Reconstructing Societies in the Aftermath of War*.
Vol 34. History.

TAMBURRI. et al., Eds. *Italian Cultural Studies 2001*. Vol 33. Essays.

ELIZABETH G. MESSINA, Ed. *In Our Own Voices*.
Vol 32. Italian/American Studies.

STANISLAO G. PUGLIESE. *Desperate Inscriptions*. Vol 31. History.

HOSTERT & TAMBURRI, Eds. *Screening Ethnicity*.
Vol 30. Italian/American Culture.

G. PARATI & B. LAWTON, Eds. *Italian Cultural Studies*. Vol 29. Essays.

HELEN BAROLINI. *More Italian Hours*. Vol 28. Fiction.

FRANCO NASI, Ed. *Intorno alla Via Emilia*. Vol 27. Culture.

ARTHUR L. CLEMENTS. *The Book of Madness & Love*. Vol 26. Poetry.

JOHN CASEY, et al. *Imagining Humanity*. Vol 25. Interdisciplinary Studies.

ROBERT LIMA. *Sardinia/Sardegna*. Vol 24. Poetry.

DANIELA GIOSEFFI. *Going On*. Vol 23. Poetry.

ROSS TALARICO. *The Journey Home*. Vol 22. Poetry.

EMANUEL DI PASQUALE. *The Silver Lake Love Poems*. Vol 21. Poetry.

JOSEPH TUSIANI. *Ethnicity*. Vol 20. Poetry.

JENNIFER LAGIER. *Second Class Citizen*. Vol 19. Poetry.

FELIX STEFANILE. *The Country of Absence*. Vol 18. Poetry.

PHILIP CANNISTRARO. *Blackshirts*. Vol 17. History.

LUIGI RUSTICHELLI, Ed. *Seminario sul racconto*. Vol 16. Narrative.

LEWIS TURCO. *Shaking the Family Tree*. Vol 15. Memoirs.

LUIGI RUSTICHELLI, Ed. *Seminario sulla drammaturgia*.
Vol 14. Theater/Essays.

FRED GARDAPHÈ. *Moustache Pete is Dead! Long Live Moustache Pete!*.
Vol 13. Oral Literature.

JONE GAILLARD CORSI. *Il libretto d'autore. 1860 - 1930*. Vol 12. Criticism.

HELEN BAROLINI. *Chiaroscuro: Essays of Identity*. Vol 11. Essays.

PICARAZZI & FEINSTEIN, Eds. *An African Harlequin in Milan*.
Vol 10. Theater/Essays.

JOSEPH RICAPITO. *Florentine Streets & Other Poems*. Vol 9. Poetry.

FRED MISURELLA. *Short Time*. Vol 8. Novella.

NED CONDINI. *Quartettsatz*. Vol 7. Poetry.

ANTHONY JULIAN TAMBURRI, Ed. *Fuori: Essays by Italian/American
Lesbiansand Gays*. Vol 6. Essays.

ANTONIO GRAMSCI. P. Verdicchio. Trans. & Intro. *The Southern Question*.
Vol 5. Social Criticism.

DANIELA GIOSEFFI. *Word Wounds & Water Flowers*. Vol 4. Poetry. $8

WILEY FEINSTEIN. *Humility's Deceit: Calvino Reading Ariosto Reading Calvino*.
Vol 3. Criticism.

PAOLO A. GIORDANO, Ed. *Joseph Tusiani: Poet. Translator. Humanist.*
  Vol 2. Criticism.
ROBERT VISCUSI. *Oration Upon the Most Recent Death of Christopher Columbus.*
  Vol 1. Poetry.